AF703801

The Complete Guide to Commercial Account Analysis and Billing

The Complete Guide to Commercial Account Analysis and Billing

Bill Andrules

CONTENTS

Copyright © 2025 by Bill Andrules
All rights reserved. No part of this book may be reproduced in any manner whatsoever without written permission except in the case of brief quotations embodied in critical articles and reviews.
First Printing, 2025

This book is dedicated to all of the commercial account analysis people in all of the financial institutions I have ever had the pleasure of working with, you know who you are. Also, to Steve and Pat Weiland who built their lifelong business around account analysis and went well out of their way to make me a part of it. To Helen Pavalko, Greg Norgord, and Jackie Micech who spent their entire adult careers advocating for account analysis, continuously promoting the concept of clear, concise, and accurate results. To Tom Hunt, Bridget Meyer, and Dan Gill who have carried the bank fee monitoring torch forward through so many years past and made the subject of bank fee monitoring a key focus for all members of the AFP-Association for Financial Professionals.

I want to also express gratitude towards the members of the original TMA 822 / Account Analysis Task Force, especially Paul Burstein and Steve Weiland, for the endless hours spent in developing and promoting standards for Account Analysis. Also, the standards created so long ago would not be as complete had it not also been for the TMA 822 / Account Analysis Review Panel that included Robert Page, Mazen Musallam, and others that I personally had the pleasure to work with in my career.

Introduction

Introducing The Complete Guide to Commercial Account Analysis. This guide will take you on an in-depth journey into the world of commercial account analysis. Whether your interest is from a banking or corporate perspective, or even that of a vendor or third-party service provider, this guide will walk you through common, best, and even some unusual practices surrounding commercial account analysis. From within a bank, this guide will provide subject matter and ideation surrounding departmental interests too. Whether a software developer looking to design actionable reporting from the bank's data warehouse, or a marketing strategist looking for new ways to increase revenue, you'll find this guide filled with actionable ideation.

The motivation for the creation of this guide came from more than 50 years of working with commercial account analysis. I was personally responsible for the successful implementation of account analysis solutions at more than 100 banks and other financial institutions during my career. Simply said, it's been my life's work.

I was inspired by colleagues along the way to create a very focused user group on LinkedIn, for those most interested in commercial account analysis. It seemed like a silly idea at first, but I created my user group in 2009 and through the years, the user group has grown to 350+ members.

This guide describes subject matter you are likely somewhat familiar with but always wanted to know more about. This guide will be a tremendous help to anyone intimately involved with account analysis, or simply someone whose work life it touches.

Information contained within this guide will help practitioners in a variety of ways, not the least of which in negotiating and/or controlling bank fees.

PART I: Implementation

Implementing an account analysis & billing system from the ground up for any financial institution can be a daunting task. A challenge like this certainly leaves one wondering where to even begin. This guide breaks down all the key components needed for a successful commercial account analysis implementation project. This part of the guide focuses on commercial banks who are billing business customers for treasury management services (aka. cash management services).

While both *treasury management* and *cash management* terms are used interchangeably in the industry, a wise person once told me that *cash management* services are simpler in nature and move funds with tools like Remote Deposit Capture, ACH, Wires, etc. whereas *treasury management* services are more complex in nature, they are made up of more sophisticated services like Lockbox, Controlled Disbursements, and Sweeps, etc.

Regardless of how you refer to them, you'll find valuable information within this guide to assist you with building (or completely revamping) the commercial billing for these services offered by a financial institution.

Implementing a new account analysis solution begins with finding one. There are many things to look for when searching for a new system, but you may find that the system you end up with simply cannot automate everything you'll find described in this book. The important thing is that having read this book, you will clearly understand exactly what you have gotten yourself into.

One

Finding a Solution

While there is a wealth of information outlined in this guide regarding the details of account analysis in general, a banker will likely find few options to choose from when searching for a commercial billing solution. A bank will likely be faced with choosing from amongst three options, option a) use the embedded commercial billing capability of the core demand deposit system already being used at the bank; b) build an entirely new commercial billing system from scratch; or c) license a separate core agnostic vendor solution designed to handle the commercial account analysis and billing functionality being sought.

Option c) may possibly require custom core integration work if integration does not already exist. Option b) will absolutely require core integration work. Option a) means the commercial analysis billing functionality is already built into the core deposit system so core integration is taken care of. When it comes to integration, all three options will require some level of integration work to deal with third party vendors, who send billing files to the account analysis system monthly.

For very small financial institutions (under $500 million in assets as an example) one may find option a) to be the best choice from an ROI-Return on Investment perspective. A small financial institution will likely have less sophisticated business customers requiring very basic needs of the commercial billing system. There are always exceptions of course and a banking customer's *need* is always going to be of upmost importance. For very small banks though, I have found that the embedded commercial billing functionality within the core deposit system(s) has for the most part been adequate and covers most of the basic billing needs. The ROI for option a) makes this the most practical choice for very small institutions.

Conversely, very large financial institutions will have very sophisticated corporate customers with very savvy treasury management departments. Ironically, some of the largest financial institutions in the world make use of custom- built or home-grown account analysis systems to meet the needs of the bank and their customers.

> *In some instances, what I call a home-grown system may have in fact evolved from a vendor solution of years gone by. It was very common to license source code when selling systems to banks back in the 1970's. Many banks enhanced these systems on their own through the years, almost to the extent they would no longer be recognized as a vendor solution from which they came to be.*

Outside of the largest banks in the world, vendor solutions (option c) are most common for a variety of reasons including industry expertise, on-going software development, software maintenance, pre-built integration, user training, and customer support.

When seeking / researching a new account analysis system, what I have discovered over time is that banks will either put together an RFP-*Request for Proposal* or hire a consulting firm to prepare the RFP for them, on their behalf. An RFP is typically sent to a few select vendors with numerous questions to be answered.

What I have found rather interesting through the years, is that these RFPs don't ask the right questions regarding account analysis (or I should say, the *hard* questions). Having answered numerous RFPs through the years, I found that RFP questions most often probed what an analysis system can do automatically vs. what the bank staff is going to be left with doing (usually manually) as a workaround. Both are important of course, but in choosing a solution, a bank really needs to understand what will be left on their shoulders after an analysis system has been implemented. A new system will certainly provide all that it is capable of, but once implemented, what needs will remain?

Even after exploring option a), b), and c) above, a bank may find themselves rather stuck using whatever commercial billing solution they currently have. In a situation such as this, this guide will likely assist in some way, with the creation of a business case for a better way forward.

Questions Every Bank Should Ask an Account Analysis Vendor

Working on the vendor side of account analysis RFPs, I have seen literally thousands of questions surrounding the subject of commercial billing. Consulting firms are often used by banks in the procurement process so it should come as no surprise that RFPs from banks sometimes look very similar to one another.

I have compiled a list through time, of what I consider to be difficult but very meaningful questions. The questions are worded so that a potential banking software vendor can simply answer them as *Yes* or *No*. One in search of a new solution may not like to see the answers to these questions, but at least there will be no surprises.

The questions I have compiled are written as though a bank is addressing the questions to a potential vendor of an account analysis system. In some cases, a vendor would want to explain themselves but nonetheless, the bank should mainly concern themselves with the simple answer of YES or NO. The questions are broken into the major subjects of Security, Operational matters, Account features, Account Relationship features, Pricing features, Account Analysis Statements, and Reporting. The entire list of questions that I feel should be included in any RFP for account analysis can be found in Appendix A: RFP Questions of Importance.

Given the options outlined in this chapter, there is a very high degree of probability that a bank will turn to a vendor solution for commercial account analysis and billing. The proposed questions outlined in Appendix A are meant to help a bank understand what they might be getting themselves into with a particular vendor solution. Different vendor systems will provide different levels of automation and synchronization with the core demand deposit system.

In the next chapter, I will dive into the building blocks of an account analysis system starting with what I call the blueprint of products and services. I have always said a builder would never even try to build a home without a detailed blueprint, nor should one try to implement an account analysis solution, without a blueprint.

Two

Designing the Blueprint of Products & Services

Before diving into the details of designing your blueprint for a new account analysis system, the following will introduce you to the AFP-Association for Financial Professionals, and the role this organization plays in account analysis.

AFP – Association for Financial Professionals

The Association for Financial Professionals is a professional society that establishes and administers standards of excellence in the industries of treasury and finance. In addition to regional conferences, the AFP hosts one of the largest networking conferences worldwide for thousands of corporate financial professionals. Originally known as the TMA (Treasury Management Association), the AFP is the original author of the *TMA Guide to Account Analysis* which established domestic standards for account analysis statements and electronic reporting via EDI-Electronic Data Interchange.

The standards developed and maintained by the AFP include both AFP Service Codes and Product Categories for financial services. For more than 30 years, the AFP Service Codes have been recognized as the industry standard for identifying service charges that appear on account analysis statements.

> *I have often referred to the AFP Service Codes as the general ledger chart of accounts for bank service fees. Unlike General ledger account numbers though, the AFP Service Codes are pre-defined for the entire industry.*

Adoption of the AFP Service Codes throughout the financial services industry has been consistent through the years. Adoption started with very large financial institutions (and corporations) but now has trickled down into commercially focused community banks, credit unions, and even what some would call small businesses. Adoption of the AFP standardization has been driven by demand from corporate America.

As you will find throughout this book, the standards established by the AFP and/or affiliated organizations cover not just the AFP Service Codes, but also the appearance of printed account analysis statements and the very detailed specifications for electronic analysis statements, both Domestic and International.

The AFP Service Codes

While they are the billing foundation in top tier banks, the AFP Service Codes are still not commonly used or shown on account analysis statements at smaller financial institutions. Whether used by a financial institution or not, one should understand that the AFP Service Codes can provide value to anyone receiving an account analysis statement. This is true whether the codes are shown on the printed image of an analysis statement, or they are delivered within an electronic file.

In 2018, a large regional bank in northern California made the strategic decision to print the assigned AFP Service Code next to every line-item service on their account analysis statements. Whether the customer is a large corporate entity or a small business, the AFP Service Code was shown on every analysis statement produced by the bank.

While smaller financial institutions typically do not make use of the AFP Service Codes and many small businesses have little or no knowledge of such, this guide will demonstrate samples of how mapping AFP Service Codes can add tremendous value to account analysis statements. Whether a financial institution starts making use of the AFP Service Codes initially or at some point in their future, this guide should serve as a resource for understanding the value of the AFP Service Codes.

Why AFP Service Codes?

All account analysis systems have a BSID - Bank Service Identification Code (aka. BTC-Bank Transaction Code, BIC-Bank Identification Code) but for the same identical service (a *Domestic Outgoing Wire* for example) there will be a different bank transaction code (and likely service description) used at each bank, thus making the BSID rather meaningless to a corporate practitioner receiving an account analysis statement from multiple banks.

The AFP Service Codes though, are all static codes, predetermined, and documented. They are designed to be mapped specifically to bank transaction codes (BSIDs). If a corporate business received analysis statements from four different banks (and they often do) and the banks displayed the AFP Service Codes on those statements, the AFP Service Code identifying a *Domestic Wire Transfer* would be the exact same AFP Service Code on all four (4) statements.

This scenario assumes of course, the banks all mapped their codes correctly. It is also important to understand that the bank service fee description for the *Wire Transfer* would likely be different from each bank. This common AFP Service Code used across all four statements then makes it rather easy, even visually, to compare pricing from one bank to another.

AFP Service Code Accreditation

For banks making use of the AFP Service Codes, the AFP offers an accreditation program that certifies the mapping of the AFP Service Codes to the bank's services/billing points (BSIDs). This AFP service includes an initial certification and then an annual review for re-certification of a bank's code mappings. A complete list of AFP accredited financial institutions is published by the AFP organization on their web site.

AFP® Association for FINANCIAL PROFESSIONALS

AFP SERVICE CODES
Accredited Provider™

Copyrighted by The Association for Financial Professionals
Printed with permission from the AFP: financialprofessionals.org

The *AFP Service Codes Accredited Provider Program* is designed to increase standardization in reporting bank compensation by recognizing banks that are using the AFP Service Codes consistently within the standard. An official logo like this shown here is licensed to banks, once their service code mappings become accredited through the AFP. The *Accredited Provider* logo is sometimes used by accredited banks on their account analysis statements, pricing brochures, RFPs, etc.

> *In 2017, a large mid-western regional bank (accredited by the AFP) was printing the accredited provider logo at the bottom of every account analysis statement produced by the bank.*

AFP Product Categories

The best practice for displaying services on account analysis statements is to show the line-item services organized within Product Categories (aka. Product Families). Think of a Product Category as a service charge *category*. Simply said, having this separation of line-item service fees makes the account analysis statement more organized, easier to read, and understand.

When the AFP Service Codes were designed, it was decided by the task force that the code would be a six-character code. The first two characters of every AFP Service Code would identify an AFP Product Category. This technique ensured that all service fees of a similar category would be sorted and/or associated together by the common category.

Not only are the AFP Service Codes uniquely identified and documented but so are the AFP Product Categories. For example, twenty-five (25) is reserved for General ACH Services. All line-item services with an AFP Service Code that starts with 25 then, belong to the General ACH Services Product Category as defined by the AFP.

Similarly, Wire and Other Funds Transfer Services would have an AFP Service Code that starts with Product Category 35. While the AFP has defined a list of standard Product Categories (and numbered / named them all), the numbers and/or the AFP defined category descriptions are not commonly used on account analysis statements at smaller community banks.

The complete list of AFP Product Categories and their numbers are AFP mapping standards and include all sorts of products. While the AFP Service Codes infer which category a line-item service fee should be included in, it is not a mandate for statement display. In many instances, I've seen *ACH Received* fees for example, shown in the Depository Services product category on a statement even though the AFP Service Code(s) start with 25. Banks do this to delineate ACH Origination items apart from ACH Received items.

While the top-tier banks will commonly show AFP Service Codes all organized by their AFP Product Category, most other commercial banks (even regional) define their own product categories, which are very similar but usually have different descriptions. I have found the following product categories to be used most often with statements at *commercially focused* banks:

Account Services
Depository Services
Remote Deposit Capture
Coin & Currency Services
ACH Origination Services
Wire Transfer Services
Fraud Prevention Services
Online Banking Services
Armored Car and Courier Services
Information Reporting Services (Balance Reporting, EDI)

Investment / Cash Management Services (Sweeps, ZBAs)
Lockbox Services
Other Third-Party Services

AFP Summary

Whether a bank is using AFP Service Codes or not, it is important to know they exist and that they can add value. The standard codes have made their way into some very small organizations for use. Overall adoption of the AFP Service Codes is widely spread. The AFP conducts ongoing training for its members along with certifications that can be achieved with advanced study.

> *I was once asked by an executive working for a large core system provider, "how is it that we have ended up with so many account analysis systems with statements that look so different?". I smiled and responded, "the people involved simply did not align themselves with the AFP and all the standards the AFP has provided for reporting in this industry".*

Blueprint Design

With every account analysis system implementation I've ever managed, I began with an empty spreadsheet workbook and started by listing the product categories that were known to be in the scope of the project. The product category list shown above was and still is a great list to start with for any account analysis implementation. I would then take each category one by one and start to add descriptions for line-item services that clearly belonged within the category.

I would typically give no concern as to whether one could in the end make a service fee functional for the bank but instead, the focus was placed on what one *would like to have*, if they could make it work.

Line-Item Services

The services within each product category have attributes that should be considered throughout the construction of any account analysis blueprint. Every service will certainly have a service description to display on the statement, but each service will also have a standard price, a bank service identification code, and most importantly a planned data source for billing data to flood the service with.

Best practice is to have a separate spreadsheet column for each of these service attributes. Eventually, all the services that end up in the blueprint will have to be populated by a volume or some other triggering mechanism from a planned data source. One should ask themself, "What is going to cause this service charge to appear on the analysis statement?". Keep in mind that when a line-item service has no volume and the charge is zero, it is typically not seen on a statement.

Another way of thinking about it is, "What is going to flood this service or trigger this service fee"? When specifying the planned data source for a service, one will likely find that many services are flooded by data from the core demand deposit system. The illustration below shows a sample blueprint with the important service attributes mentioned here.

Service Blueprint - First National Bank of Your Town

AFP Service Code Mapping	Product Category	Bank Service ID Code	Statement Description	Balance Based	Volume Based	File Posting Frequency	Unit Price	Billing Source
	DEP		* Depository Services					
	DEP		Account Maintenance Fee		Yes		15.0000	Auto-Generated
	DEP		Deposits		Yes	Daily	0.7500	Core DDA Interface File
	DEP		Deposited Items		Yes	Daily	0.1500	Core DDA Interface File
	DEP		Paid Checks		Yes	Daily	0.2200	Core DDA Interface File
	DEP		Balance Assessment Fee	Yes			0.1300	System Generated
			* ACH Origination Services					
250000	ACH	1076	ACH Monthly Maintenance		Yes			Auto-Generated for Accounts who Subscribe
	ACH	1089	ACH Re-deposited Items		Yes	Monthly	1.5000	Back Office ACH Billing File
250501	ACH	1076	ACH Transmissions Per File		Yes	Monthly	10.0000	Back Office ACH Billing File
	ACH	1254	ACH Items Deleted		Yes	Monthly	15.0000	Back Office ACH Billing File

To create a professional looking account analysis statement in the end, one must consider many minor details as they relate to describing services within the blueprint. One could certainly begin by listing services within categories using any service description, but the goal should be to develop the actual service description that would eventually appear on the account analysis statement or possibly on a banking brochure / pricing proposal. Listed below are some initial guidelines for creating a professional blueprint of products and services.

Service Descriptions

Abbreviations

While abbreviating words may leave one guessing, it is commonly required when building a services blueprint. The reason is most account analysis systems have limitations as to just how long a service description can be. In other words: "Online Domestic Outgoing Wire Transfer – Recurring" may or may not fit on the account analysis statement. Abbreviation is often the first thing one turns to in a situation like this. The most important thing to remember is that if you are going to abbreviate, you should do so in a 100% consistent manner throughout the blueprint.

> *During one implementation project in Ontario CA, a bank built a blueprint of 300+ line-item services. Using their existing blueprint to start with, the bank found that existing service descriptions contained what was supposed to be the word CHECK on numerous line-item service billing points. The problem was the word CHECK was abbreviated 5 different ways within the blueprint (e.g. CHK, CHEK, CK, CHCK, CHKS).*

Pluralization

Service descriptions often describe bank fees/charges based upon a volume count. Consistency in pluralization is important when describing such services. Shown below is an example of service descriptions that are not consistent.

Description	Volume	Unit Price	Service Charge
* Wire Transfer Services			
Online Outgoing Domestic Wire	6	12.5000	$ 75.00
Online Outgoing International Wires	4	35.0000	$ 140.00

If consistent throughout the blueprint, either of the above approaches could be used (Wire or Wires) but mixing the approaches within the same blueprint shows a lack of attention to detail and is the beginning of customers starting to question other aspects of their billing.

Punctuation

Using punctuation in service descriptions can help differentiate one version of a service from another as in the sample below:

Description	Volume	Unit Price	Service Charge
* Wire Transfer Services			
Domestic Outgoing Wire - Recurring	4	20.0000	$ 80.00
Domestic Outgoing Wire	2	25.0000	$ 50.00

Notice the spacing around the punctuation above. A more professional appearance is achieved if any such use of a dash (in this example) has the exact spacing throughout. In the sample below we see mixed punctuation (a dash vs. a slash) which should always be avoided.

Description	Volume	Unit Price	Service Charge
* Wire Transfer Services			
Online Outgoing Domestic Wire - Recurring	6	10.0000	$ 60.00
Online Outgoing Domestic Wire	6	12.0000	$ 72.00
Online Outgoing International Wire	4	25.0000	$ 100.00
Domestic Outgoing Wire / Recurring	4	20.0000	$ 80.00

Capitalization

As with all descriptions, consistency is most important but thought needs to be given to the *case* of words as well. There is no correct case except consistent usage. Many banks use *Proper Case* but there is no right or wrong answer. Shown below is an example of what not to do.

Description	Volume	Unit Price	Service Charge
* Wire Transfer Services			
Domestic outgoing wire - recurring	4	20.0000	$ 80.00
Domestic Outgoing Wire	2	25.0000	$ 50.00

Consideration also needs to be given to acronyms. Having both **ACH Credits** and **Ach Debits** in the same blueprint depicts an unprofessional image, or at the very least something far from perfect.

Beyond Service Descriptions

Listing all service descriptions within each product category will be a great start to any blueprint construction. The initial process will leave one wondering about whether the list is complete or not. I have always advocated for including every possible service imaginable without concern for how the charge will be generated (or even if the charge will initially be generated). Time, effort, and creativity, will determine if a service makes it to the planned destination (which is on the account analysis statement and in the bank's revenue stream).

> *During one implementation project at a large commercial bank in downtown Portland OR, the product manager told me he wanted three (3) line-item services added to every single product category whether they ever use them or not. The services were a Monthly Maintenance Fee, a One Time Implementation Fee, and an on-demand Training Fee. In every single implementation I was ever involved with after that event, I made the same suggestion to every bank I ever visited.*

As each line-item service is added to the blueprint (which is still just a spreadsheet at this point), one should also assign as many of the service attributes as possible to the service. As previously mentioned, service attributes go beyond standard unit price. If you will be using AFP Service Codes, what AFP Service Code will you assign to each service? What cost are you going to assign to each service (if any)? What will you have for a display sequence of each line-item service within the product category? What will be the overall display sequence of all the product categories?

The bank staff will become familiar with the display sequence of products and services over time so choosing a logical presentation sequence will help make your implementation of the analysis system more intuitive. For example, you might consider putting all fees regarding monthly maintenance at the very top as the first line-item in the display of each product category.

Next, we will dive a little deeper into the building of your service blueprint with two sample Product Categories (ACH Origination and Wire Transfers). The detailed considerations shown below would be similar (but different) for every single product category in your eventual blueprint of services (aka. The Product Catalogue).

ACH Origination Services

This suggested product family of services is used to categorize charges for those services provided by the bank's ACH Department. **ACH Origination Services** is the most common description I've seen used for this category on account analysis statements.

> *The official AFP category description for these services would be* ***General ACH Services****. When setting up statement descriptions / legends for your account analysis system though, it is not mandatory to use the AFP defined category description.*

A suggested statement view for a list of commonly used ACH services is shown below.

Service Detail

Description	Volume	Unit Price	Service Charge	Balance Equivalent
* ACH Origination Services				
ACH Origination Module Maintenance	1	50.0000	$ 50.00	$ 325,893
ACH Debits Originated	23	0.2000	$ 4.60	$ 29,982
ACH Credits Originated	245	0.2000	$ 49.00	$ 319,375
ACH Addendas Originated	4	0.2500	$ 1.00	$ 6,518
ACH Items - Same Day Surcharge	5	1.0000	$ 5.00	$ 32,589
ACH Returns	2	5.0000	$ 10.00	$ 65,179
ACH Re-deposited Items	6	1.5000	$ 9.00	$ 58,661
ACH Transmissions Per File	4	10.0000	$ 40.00	$ 260,714
ACH Items Deleted	56	15.0000	$ 840.00	$ 5,475,002
ACH Files Deleted	1	40.0000	$ 40.00	$ 260,714
ACH Items Reversed	7	15.0000	$ 105.00	$ 684,375
ACH Files Reversed	2	40.0000	$ 80.00	$ 521,429
ACH Notification of Change	2	2.0000	$ 4.00	$ 26,071

The example illustration shown above is a granular version of commonly used ACH Origination services.

Granularity

Many community bank service blueprints would likely not contain the service granularity shown in the statement view example above. The more granular items are shown here for price comparisons and to illustrate what may be possible. The charge for *ACH Files* is a good example. Some account analysis blueprints would simply have a line item called *ACH Files* and charge 5.00 – 10.00 per/file. In the example above, you can see a separate charge for Files Deleted and Files Reversed. Charging for *ACH File Transmissions* is very common, charging for Files Deleted and Files Reversed is not nearly as common.

Granularity of billing for these services is often dictated by the data source for the billing. If a bank is using an automated back-office ACH Origination tool as the *system of record* for billing volumes, there is a good chance one will be able to easily identify granular differences like an item deletion, a batch deletion, or a file deletion. At times, banks find themselves keeping track of such activities manually or on a spreadsheet and then uploading that billing data into their account analysis system at the end of a month. In this scenario, granularity becomes cumbersome and costly, and in some instances, almost unrealistic.

Obtaining ACH billing data from a core deposit system normally leaves one with only debit / credit transaction counts. Billing for ACH Notifications of Change (NOCs), ACH Files, and ACH Addenda records can become very challenging. Typically, a core deposit system will not have this ACH information readily available within because these are not debits or credits (but they are still what I refer to as, "service chargeable events").

The services listed below would depict a very common display of ACH Origination service fees at a smaller community bank without a sophisticated / automated ACH back-office processing system.

Service Detail

Description	Volume	Unit Price	Service Charge	Balance Equivalent
* ACH Origination Services				
ACH Origination Module Maintenance	1	50.0000	$ 50.00	$ 325,893
ACH Debits Originated	23	0.2000	$ 4.60	$ 29,982
ACH Credits Originated	245	0.2000	$ 49.00	$ 319,375
ACH Transmissions Per File	4	10.0000	$ 40.00	$ 260,714

Pricing

When it comes to ACH Origination service fees, there are pricing observations that can be made regardless of the actual unit price being used. For example, ACH Originated Items are almost always set to the same unit price whether they are debits or credits. In fact, a bank will commonly have a single line-item fee called ACH Items and lump credits and debits together. Best practice is to provide granularity.

AFP Coding for ACH Origination Services

The AFP Service Code mapping for the Product Category known as *General ACH Services* provides detailed options based on the granularity of a bank's blueprint. *ACH Returns* for example allows one to map different AFP Service Codes for debits and credits, but the standard also provides a mapping option for having a single line-item charge for *ACH Returns* (a combined volume of debits and credits). Community banks do not often have separate line-item charges for *ACH Debit / Credit Returns* so charges for such Returns are most often shown as a single line-item.

A sample AFP Service Code mapping for AFP Product Category 25 is shown in the illustration below. Actual AFP Service Codes are copyrighted material, but the few codes shown here are being shared with permission from the AFP.

Service Detail					
AFP Code	Description	Volume	Unit Price	Service Charge	Balance Equivalent
	* ACH Origination Services				
250000	ACH Origination Module Maintenance	1	50.0000	$ 50.00	$ 325,893
250100	ACH Debits Originated	23	0.2000	$ 4.60	$ 29,982
250101	ACH Credits Originated	245	0.2000	$ 49.00	$ 319,375
250501	ACH Transmissions Per File	4	10.0000	$ 40.00	$ 260,714

While *ACH Received* items (debits and credits) have AFP Service Codes that start with 25 and are technically a part of *General ACH Services*, these *Received* service charges are most often placed among the Depository Services category on account analysis statements from community banks.

Very large financial institutions tend to follow strict AFP standards, showing the AFP Service Code along with each bank description in AFP Service Code order. Community Banks tend to deviate from this display by hiding the AFP Service Code and putting service charge line items wherever the bank feels best understood by their customers, based upon the bank pricing brochures, proposals, and the general opinion of the bank's Treasury Sales management.

For every AFP Service Code defined, there is an AFP suggested description for statement display but also a more detailed description that can be used by licensed users of the AFP Service Codes. Below is a sample of some AFP Service Codes for ACH Origination along with the AFP suggested service description (for statements) and the more detailed service description intended to more thoroughly document the code's purpose. These codes below are copyrighted material but are being shared here with permission from the AFP.

AFP Service Code 250000

General ACH Maintenance

Charge for providing ACH funds transfer services, excluding concentration and automated funding services. This is often a fixed charge.

AFP Service Code 250100

ACH Originated-Debit

Charge for processing an ACH debit transaction initiated by the customer.

AFP Service Code 250101

ACH Originated-Credit

Charge for processing an ACH credit transaction initiated by the customer.

AFP Service Code 250501

ACH-Input-Auto Transmission

Charge for processing a file containing ACH transaction detail received from the customer via data transmission.

Wire Transfer Services

This product category of services is used to delineate charges for those services provided by a bank's Wire Transfer department (e.g. the *Wire Room*). The AFP category for these services would be Product Code 35 - *Wire and Other Funds Transfer Services.*

The suggested statement view for a list of commonly used wire transfer services is shown below. This is a very granular version of common wire transfer services.

Description	Volume	Unit Price	Service Charge	Balance Equivalent
* **Wire Transfer Services**				
Wire Transfer Module Maintenance	1	50.0000	$ 50.00	$ 325,893
Online Outgoing Domestic Wire - Recurring	6	10.0000	$ 60.00	$ 391,072
Online Outgoing Domestic Wire	6	12.5000	$ 75.00	$ 488,840
Online Outgoing International Wire	4	20.0000	$ 80.00	$ 521,429
Domestic Outgoing Wire - Recurring	4	20.0000	$ 80.00	$ 521,429
Domestic Outgoing Wire	2	25.0000	$ 50.00	$ 325,893
International Outgoing Wire USD - Recurring	4	35.0000	$ 140.00	$ 912,500
International Outgoing Wire FX - Recurring	4	25.0000	$ 100.00	$ 651,786
International Outgoing Wire USD	4	40.0000	$ 160.00	$ 1,042,858
International Outgoing Wire FX	4	30.0000	$ 120.00	$ 782,143
Domestic Incoming Wire	3	15.0000	$ 45.00	$ 293,304
International Incoming Wire	6	15.0000	$ 90.00	$ 586,607
Wire Notification - Phone	1	4.0000	$ 4.00	Waived
Wire Notification - eMail	1	0.1000	$ 0.10	$ 652
Wire Notification - Fax	1	0.3000	$ 0.30	$ 1,955
Wire Notification - Other	1	5.0000	$ 5.00	$ 32,589
Domestic Wire Investigation Tracer	1	20.0000	$ 20.00	$ 130,357
International Wire Investigation Tracer	1	30.0000	$ 30.00	$ 195,536
Wire Transfer Module Setup Fee	1	100.0000	$ 100.00	Fee Based

Granularity

Many community bank blueprints would not contain the detailed service granularity shown in the illustration above. The more granular items are shown here for price comparisons and to illustrate what may be possible. Wire Notifications is a good example, some account analysis blueprints would simply have a line item called "*Wire Advice(s)*" and charge approximately 2.00 per/advice. In the example above, you can see a unique fee structure for each type of wire advice.

General Pricing Observations - Wire Transfer Services

While all bank blueprints for wires tend to break out Domestic vs. International and Incoming vs. Outgoing wires, the *Recurring* or *Repetitive* wires are not commonly priced separately by community banks. Even though a recurring wire is a bit easier and should cost a bank less to create for a customer, the account analysis pricing is not commonly set to a lower unit price as shown above.

Granularity of billing for these services is often dictated by the data source for billing. If the wire system is the *system of record* for billing volumes, there is a good chance one will be able to identify a recurring wire or an international wire using FX vs. USD from the billing source.

If the wire billing data is being extracted from the core deposit system, then the wire identity may not be so clear, and a bank would be forced into a less granular wires billing blueprint. In general, smaller banks tend to have less granular billing blueprints.

The services listed below would depict a very common display of wire transfer services at a smaller community bank. The AFP Service Codes shown below are copyrighted material but are being shared here with permission from the AFP.

Service Detail					
AFP Code	Description	Volume	Unit Price	Service Charge	Balance Equivalent
	* Wire Transfer Services				
350000	Wire Transfer Module Maintenance	1	50.0000	$ 50.00	$ 325,893
	Online Outgoing Domestic Wire	6	12.5000	$ 75.00	$ 488,840
	Online Outgoing International Wire	4	20.0000	$ 80.00	$ 521,429
350202	Domestic Outgoing Wire	2	25.0000	$ 50.00	$ 325,893
350212	International Outgoing Wire	4	30.0000	$ 120.00	$ 782,143
350300	Domestic Incoming Wire	3	15.0000	$ 45.00	$ 293,304
350310	International Incoming Wire	6	15.0000	$ 90.00	$ 586,607
	Wire Advice	4	4.0000	$ 16.00	Waived
	Wire Transfer Module Setup Fee	1	100.0000	$ 100.00	Fee Based

Note that all *Wire Advice(s)* are now lumped into a single fee regardless of how the notification / advice was delivered. This blueprint shows a single unit price for Domestic Outgoing Wires whether it is a repetitive wire or not.

Best practice would be to not get too general or vague with wire fees. Some banks don't have a separate *Online* wire fee for example. The problem with this is that an online wire should in fact cost a customer less than a more manual wire. If a bank doesn't break them out, the customer often suffers the consequence of paying too much for an online wire. The bank also suffers though, from an inability to be competitive with their pricing.

Pricing

When it comes to wire fees, there are observations that can be made regardless of the actual unit price being used. For example, an International Wire is almost always set to a higher unit price than a Domestic Wire of the same type. Another observation would be Online wires, the unit prices for such are almost always set to a lower unit price than a wire done by any other means. Community banks do this to create the desired behavior of having the customer process their wire via the online banking platform in use.

> In 2017 a community bank observed customers were continuing to create outgoing wires manually even though they could do so with their online banking platform. Using account analysis billing data, the bank created a list of these customers and decided to invite them all to a special training session for online banking. They created their roster of customers by looking at account analysis statements to see who had a line item shown for an online banking maintenance fee but then only manual (vs. online) wires shown on the same statement.

International wires often show two service charge line items, one involves USD and the other FX – Foreign Exchange. While the unit prices for these wires are often the same, this delineation allows a bank to charge a higher unit price for one of them. Observations have shown that the USD version of an international wire is often the same or less than the FX version, but case review has proven there is no clear consistency with this price differentiation.

A final observation of pricing for wires would be that incoming wire fees, whether they be domestic or international, are typically the same unit price.

AFP Coding for Wire Transfer Services

The AFP coding for AFP Product Category 35 delineates *Automated* wires from *Manual* wires. Think of this delineation as wires done in an online banking system vs. any other means. The AFP Service

Code mapping also gets very detailed when it comes to recurring wires. Normally Domestic Outgoing Wires would all be coded with AFP Service Code 350202 and this would be the default mapping. If you are using separate service coding for *Recurring* wires however, the AFP codes vary a bit to decipher how much information is really being duplicated in a template with the recurring wire. A recurring wire might be looked at from an AFP mapping perspective as completely repetitive vs. semi-repetitive. As previously mentioned, community banks do not often have separate unit prices for recurring wires.

A sample of the wire transfer AFP Codes shown in the service samples above, are defined by the AFP as follows. These codes below are copyrighted material but are being shared here with permission from the AFP.

AFP Service Code 350000

Funds Transfer System Maintenance

Charge for providing funds transfer services. This is often a fixed charge.

AFP Service Code 350202

Domestic Outgoing Wire

Charge for processing a wire transfer initiated by telephone, letter, or other non-electronic mode where the debit account is pre-set but the transferred dollar amount and the credit instructions may vary.

AFP Service Code 350212

International Outgoing Wire

Charge for processing a wire transfer to a CHIPS member bank initiated by telephone, letter, or other non-electronic mode where the debit account is pre-set but the transferred dollar amount and the credit instructions may vary.

AFP Service Code 350300

Domestic Incoming Wire

Charge for posting and handling a Fedwire transfer received for the customer's account.

AFP Service Code 350310

International Incoming Wire

Charge for posting and handling a CHIPS transfer received for the customer's account.

Summary

Building your blueprint for a new or re-implementation of an account analysis system is perhaps the most important step of the entire implementation process. Everything that is produced by the account analysis system will be based upon the blueprint of product categories and line-item services defined within the blueprint. If a service is not in the blueprint, it will not exist in account analysis. This is why I advocate for the inclusion of every possible line-item service (and category) anticipated by the bank. Most account analysis systems have user friendly options for dealing with services that are simply not being used.

Three

Accounts & Relationships

Much of the complexity surrounding account analysis most certainly comes from the construction of account relationships and the creation of analysis results for each relationship. As it turns out, there is a desire in commercial billing to put deposit accounts for a business together into a relationship of accounts for billing purposes. This concept of a relationship structure provides the ability to set pricing and rates for the relationship of accounts as one account, versus billing a company for each individual deposit account separately.

The benefits of relationship summary billing are that account balances and activity volumes can be aggregated together so that better overall pricing can be achieved for a customer. Banks will often provide higher earnings allowance rates for higher balances and lower per/unit pricing for higher service volumes. A collection of accounts all aggregated together will stand a great chance of reaching balances levels and volume levels needed for preferred pricing because all the accounts of a customer are combined into one.

Account Linkage

Every account analysis system works a bit differently when it comes to constructing account relationships, but a common approach involves using what I call a separate *Relationship Summary Account*. Some systems refer to these relationship summary accounts as group accounts, composite accounts, etc. but whatever they are called, they represent a summary or consolidation of all the customer's demand deposit accounts (both balances and services) linked to the *Relationship Summary Account.*

Imagine three demand deposit accounts for a company that are going to be linked together into a relationship summary for account analysis and billing. In this example, assume the account numbers are 111, 222, and 333. To link these accounts together, a fourth account (a relationship summary) would be required by most analysis systems and the deposit accounts would all point at that fourth account because it is the relationship summary account, or what I like to call the tie that binds.

Relationship Summary Accounts typically come with a code in front of the account number to indicate it is not a real deposit account, but instead a relationship summary record. A Family relationship summary account would for example, have a code of "F" in front of the account number.

Account Number	Customer Name		Relationship Parent	Parent Name
111	Alpha Insurance Payroll	Linked to:	F 333	Alpha Insurance
222	Alpha Insurance Operating	Linked to:	F 333	Alpha Insurance
333	Alpha Insurance	Linked to:	F 333	Alpha Insurance
F 333	Alpha Insurance Corp			

The family relationship of accounts shown above is one of the most common structures used in account analysis when dealing with family relationships (sometimes referred to as Composites or Groups). Remember that 111, 222, and 333 are real checking account numbers. F 333 was used because 333 is considered the family parent. Account 333 in this scenario is the deposit account that will pay for all the fees in the account analysis relationship.

While many banks used this structure through the years, a flaw in the design surfaced and created cause for re-design. Problems arose with this original design in analysis because deposit account 333 would one day have to be closed for some reason, usually check fraud. With account 333 closed, a new parent would need to be created, account 444 for example. The problem now is that a bank needed to create a new relationship summary for the new parent 444. So, F 444 was added to the system and the operations department would literally have to de-link accounts from F 333 and re-link them to a new relationship summary account known as F 444.

What is described above, became one of the most arduous tasks in the account analysis operations department. Fortunately, there was a simple answer to the problem and most banks (including their software vendors) have migrated to a new design. The idea is to simply use a token account number or what I call a *pseudo* account number for the relationship summary account and then link all the deposit accounts to it. This meant software changes so that relationship summary account records could separately store what became known as the *chargeable* account number in analysis. Today, account relationships look very much like what is shown here below:

Account Number	Customer Name		Relationship Parent	Parent Name
111	Alpha Insurance Payroll	Linked to:	F 01	Alpha Insurance
222	Alpha Insurance Operating	Linked to:	F 01	Alpha Insurance
333	Alpha Insurance	Linked to:	F 01	Alpha Insurance
F 01	Alpha Insurance Corp	Charges to:	333	

> In the late 1980's I visited a very large west coast bank that specialized in venture capital business accounts. The account analysis operations team was very frustrated by how much time they spent de-linking and re-linking deposit accounts every month. At first, I had no idea what they were talking about but by the end of the day, it was clear to me that the way relationships were commonly constructed had to change. By the 1990's most banks (and software vendors) reverted to the alternative design of relationship structures shown above, but there is little doubt in my mind, that there are banks out there today with older analysis systems and they are still de-linking and re-linking deposit accounts whenever a parent account is closed for check fraud.

Blending Balances and Services

When generating analysis results for a relationship of two or more deposit accounts, analysis systems have lots of data to be concerned with. What if one of the customer accounts in the relationship had special pricing for some of their services? Do all accounts in the relationship use the exact same price for a given service code? Do all the deposit accounts in a relationship have the same earnings allowance rate? Is it possible that one of the deposit accounts earned interest for their balance in the deposit system? Each of these situations and more, need to be accounted for when generating the calculated results of analysis at the relationship summary level.

More advanced analysis systems in the industry have calculation options controlling how deposit accounts are rolled up together into one relationship summary. In fact, you will likely find systems referring to data fields called *rollup code* or *blending option.* Regardless of what they are called, they control how volumes, charges, earnings allowance, and account balances might be aggregated together into a relationship summary billing statement.

Blending Services

When a customer relationship of accounts uses blended pricing for services, then for each given service the analysis system will add the service volumes together and form the relationship total volume for the service. Typically, the calculation of *volume X unit price* is then done at the summary level. In essence, all deposit accounts are getting the same unit price for the service because the service is using blended pricing.

The price to use for each service is determined at the relationship summary level. In the case of a service that is not blended, an analysis system will calculate the *volume X unit price* for each service and deposit account at the detail account level and then add up the resulting charges of those calculations. In this case, each deposit account determines its' own price, and the resulting charges are added up to form the relationship summary total.

Best practice in the industry is to have the relationship summary account drive the service pricing and do the *volume X unit price* calculation where service blending is used. Having different unit prices for the same service within a relationship will typically lead to confusion and phone calls as to why the situation exists.

When the situation does exist, analysis systems struggle with "what price to show on the summary statement" because the underlying deposit accounts have different unit pricing for the same service. Some analysis systems will divide the total charges by the total volume and print the average unit price on the summary statement.

Service Detail					
Statement Account	Description	Volume	Unit Price	Service Charge	
111	Paid Checks Service	5	0.2200	$ 1.10	
222	Paid Checks Service	7	0.1500	$ 1.05	
333	Paid Checks Service	9	0.2200	$ 1.98	
F 01	Paid Checks Service	21	0.1967	$ 4.13	

Other systems simply will not show a unit price on the relationship summary statement at all:

333	Paid Checks Service		9	0.2200	$ 1.98
F01	Paid Checks Service		21		$ 4.13

Best practice is for the analysis system to show a separate statement line for each distinct service unit price on the relationship summary statement, along with the associated volume charged at that unit price. This technique makes it very clear that a single service is using different unit pricing on subsidiary accounts. In this case, the summary statement would look like this for the *Paid Checks* service:

Service Detail					
Statement Account	Description	Volume	Unit Price	Service Charge	
F 01	Paid Checks Service	14	0.2200	$ 3.08	
F 01	Paid Checks Service	7	0.1500	$ 1.05	

Blending Balances

Blending balances in account analysis presents some of the same challenges as blending services but the blending is very focused on specific balances for specific reasons vs. dealing with what could be hundreds of distinct line-item services. One of the most common balances to be dealt with in account analysis is the NIF-Net Investable Funds, the balance upon which the earnings allowance is calculated for each account.

Blending here refers to whether the system should calculate an earnings allowance for each deposit account and sum up the earnings allowance for use at the relationship summary level or sum up all the investable balances from all the deposit accounts in the relationship and then calculate earnings allowance at the relationship summary level. In essence, each account is benefiting from the exact same earnings allowance rate when balances are blended like this.

If balance blending is not used, each deposit account potentially has an earnings allowance calculated on its' own, and the earnings rates could vary. Just like the case with service blending, the result is divided by the basis. In this case the earnings allowance total is divided by the

Net Investable Balance to determine the overall effective rate. Again, this can be confusing to a customer as shown here:

Statement Account	Net Investable Funds		Earnings Rate	Earnings Allowance		
111	$	20,500.00	0.0500%	0.84		
222	$	25,000.00	0.0700%	1.44		
333	$	30,000.00	0.0400%	0.99		
F01	$	75,500.00	0.0527%	3.27		

Another area where balance blending comes into play is uncollected funds. Uncollected funds fees are designed to be calculated and charged whenever an account draws into uncollected funds on any day of the month. With relationship structures however, one may expect to have an entire relationship of accounts looked at as a single customer when trying to determine if a customer is in fact, drawing into the total uncollected balance.

Some account analysis systems are aware of a daily relationship summary balance on any given day of the month, but most are not. Some systems can only see the daily balance history for a single account, even if it is in a relationship structure.

Establishing Relationship Summary Accounts

When implementing account relationships in analysis, it is important to understand the concept of linking accounts together. It is also important to understand some of the complexity behind producing analysis results when accounts are linked together. The concepts described above almost always physically include a relationship summary account record. This account record has a name and address, a complete set of demographics, and usually some other account record settings controlling how subsidiary account results from analysis are all combined.

Relationship summary account information is typically copied from one of the primary deposit account records. This way, the name and address for the summary statement can contain the same (copied) address as the primary account in the relationship. The copying of information almost always happens automatically. Some systems will require the primary account to be the same account that is being charged for all of the fees in the relationship. Other systems will allow a user to stipulate a primary (or key) account to be used when copying such information. Suffice to say relationship summary accounts are just like deposit accounts as they contain a mailing address, a branch, a cost center, an account type, etc.

Because the copying of this critical information is automatic with relationship summary accounts, it is the linkage of the relationship structures that is most important. When implementing an account analysis system, the most common practice is to export any/all existing relationship structure(s) and import them into the new system. Certainly, such could be done manually with the GUI of an analysis system but due to volume involved, this step is almost always done with an ETL-Extract, Transform, and Load process using MS Excel files.

Four

Account Analysis Statements

I often say in presentations, "where else from within the bank, can you pick up a piece of paper, and instantly see everything a business customer is doing with the bank?". This is what the account analysis statement is all about. Some call the statement a report because it is broken into sections and delivers varying types of information. If one were to name a single area of commercial billing where bank customers and bank staff come together, it would have to be in reviewing customer statements and analysing results.

History of the Account Analysis Statement

Account analysis statements were not initially designed to be given to customers, they were "*internal only*" documents for bankers to understand the profitability of a customer when considering an account balance alongside bank fees being paid by the customer (if any). It wasn't until the mid-1970's did these profitability statements start landing in the hands of large corporate customers (and every bank's version of these internal bank reports looked quite a bit different). Imagine a large oil & gas company receiving and then interpreting these documents from different banks they worked with.

A task force was formed almost four decades ago by what was then called the National Corporate Cash Management Association (NC-CMA), today known as the Association for Financial Professionals

(AFP). This task force consisted of 11 people and represented vendors, banks, and corporate practitioners. Their goal was to define a clear and consistent format for bank account analysis reporting. Together, the task force created the original standards for the account analysis statement.

Once the account analysis standards became known (even before they were officially published), various software vendors and banks went to work developing / modifying account analysis software to conform to the standards. This development was easier said than done as everyone involved had their own interpretation of the standards.

The work of the task force resulted in a publication then known as the *TMA Guide to Account Analysis* (aka. *The Green Book*). The book was titled the *TMA Guide to Account Analysis* because the NCCMA changed its' name to the TMA-Treasury Management Association in the late 1980's before finally settling on AFP.

The *TMA Guide to Account Analysis* was very focused on an EDI (Electronic Data Interchange) format for account analysis known as EDI Transaction Set 822. The guide also though, produced sample statements for the new account analysis standards, what I have always called the *paper statement standard for account analysis*. I have always used this term *paper statement* to differentiate from the electronic version of account analysis. Ironically, few banks still print account analysis statements and mail them due to production costs and postage expense, but I still sometimes refer to the AFP standards as *paper statement* standards.

There were two major challenges for the industry presented by the new account analysis standards. One was the statement image itself (aka. the printed statement). Software in the industry needed to produce the statement image in accordance with the standards (regardless of individual interpretations).

The second challenge was the construction of the EDI Transaction Set 822 file which represented a digital version of the account analysis statement. The initial problem was there were no software systems available to create this EDI 822 file format. This file format eventually became the domestic standard for account analysis and based on this file format, bank fee monitoring systems were born. Imagine an insurance conglomerate paying $1m per/year in bank fees, being able to ingest EDI 822 files from banking partners, so that the fees from individual banks could be digitally compared.

> *As a contract programmer back in the 1980's, I was asked to develop a system that would take account analysis data from any core banking system and create an EDI Transaction Set 822 file. The EDI file would eventually be consumed by corporate systems to do automated bank fee monitoring within corporate treasury. Given this opportunity, I created one of the very first software applications for a bank to create a TS 822 file. The system ended up being used at some of the largest banks in the country and was then known as "The 822 Express". Because the TMA standards were subject to interpretation, there were multiple interpretations for the EDI 822 files being created by banks. I am to this day very proud of the fact that the 822 files created by "The 822 Express", became known as being amongst the cleanest and purest renditions of the documented TMA standards, in the entire industry.*

One of the requirements for development of "*The 822 Express*" was that it needed to accept analysis results from any account analysis system and then turn those results into an EDI 822 file. This requirement meant that "*The 822 Express*" needed to ingest analysis data from various systems, so a standard record format was needed for transmitting analysis data to "*The 822 Express*". The *ADF-Analysis Data File* was designed and developed by Stephen J. Weiland of the Weiland Financial Group (one of many Steve's contributions to the world of bank fee monitoring). The ADF is still in use today, licensed by software vendors and also some of the largest banks in the country. The ADF file format, made the creation of "*The 822 Express*" possible.

While its original design was an "*internal only*" document to describe in detail, the cost of doing business with the bank, modernization through the years has allowed the account analysis statement to be delivered to customers in multiple ways. The analysis statement is now even used in marketing / advertising of treasury management services.

The analysis statement truly is that one piece of paper showing not only what treasury services a business customer is using at a bank, it also clearly depicts what banking services a business customer is not (yet) using.

Statement Templates

The branding on account analysis statements is very important for banks because this monthly report is the primary communication between the bank and their commercial clients. When we think about analysis statements and their overall appearance, the bank has probably already made a significant investment in the design components of their checking account (Demand Deposit) statements. Therefore, the appearance of the account analysis statement should follow the overall branding components of the DDA statement. Certainly, the analysis statement contains different information on it but the fonts, colors, logos, shading, borders, etc. should appear as if the analysis statement is coming from the same bank.

A bank may have different types of accounts that would warrant certain information left off (or included in) an analysis statement. A best practice for account analysis would be to use a statement template approach where each statement template represents something unique about the information being shown for a particular customer. A sample of two very distinct templates in analysis would be one designed for a commercial analyzed account and another for a non-analyzed (aka. fee-based) account. A fee-based design is common for small business accounts in the treasury management industry because they do not normally have an earnings credit rate assigned to them. Without an earnings allowance, a billing statement appears more simplistic because there aren't any compensating balance / balance requirement stipulations on such statements.

Another reason I advocate for different statement templates for different types of accounts has to do with the content of entire sections of a statement. A customer billed by invoice vs. auto-debiting would likely have an invoice section for their account analysis. A bank may want to show historical billing data for certain types of accounts (like accounts with an annual billing compensation cycle). Whatever the case may be, using a template approach (and a system supporting multiple templates) will give the bank the ultimate flexibility in the final image of their account analysis report to their commercial customer.

Statement Design

When you look at the statement design for account analysis, understanding the various sections of the statement will seem less intimidating when you consider each section as separate and distinct. The following statement sections are commonly used in account analysis.

- Page Header (Account Identification & Mailing Address)
- Page Footer
- Relationship Summary Accounts
- Balance Summary (Computation)
- Compensation (Results of Analysis / Account Position)
- Service Detail & Summary
- Balance Requirement Messaging
- Historical Performance (History)

Page Header

The Page Header section is typically where one would see the bank's logo, account identifying information, and the customer's name and address. Banks are typically not mailing analysis statements anymore but instead, providing access to them via online banking portals. As such, there is no real need for the complete mailing address of an account to be shown. In essence, a statement design could re-use this page real estate in other ways. A mailing address alone often takes up to six printed lines (about one inch in depth) and as much as four inches across the page, or the size of a normal window on a window envelope.

Page 1 of 4

Your National Bank

Statement Ending: June 30th, 2025
Account Number: Account: F 3333
Contact: Jeff Davis
Phone Number: (800) 123-4567

Alpha Betta Industries
Accounting
123 Any Street
Your Town, USA 98765-4321

ACCOUNT ANALYSIS STATEMENT

FOR THE PERIOD 06/01/2025 THROUGH 06/30/2025

Page Footer

The page footer for an account analysis statement is a great location to place other contact information for the customer such as the banks web site, mailing address, and a more generic phone number. This is also a good place to incorporate other logos such as that of the FDIC.

Member FDIC Your National Bank | PO Box 12345 | Wellington, FL 33414 (800) 123-4567 | www.yourbank.com | Member FDIC AFP SERVICE CODES Accredited Provider

The AFP has a logo for bank use designating that a bank is an accredited provider of the AFP Service Codes (covered in another chapter). To use this logo from the AFP the bank needs to be in fact, an accredited / licensed provider of the AFP Service Codes.

Bank Messaging or Advertising

Now that banks are not commonly printing and mailing account analysis statements (due to the high cost of production and mailing) some banks have begun to use these statements for marketing purposes. Imagine the analysis system seeing that a customer is not using the bank's remote deposit capture service. Also imagine that the analysis system can see that the customer is depositing more than just a few checks each month by bringing them to a branch. Wouldn't it be a great opportunity to put information about the bank's RDC service on the analysis statement for the customer? This is just one marketing method being used, now that the cost of printing and mailing has been eliminated. Consider the following advertising on page 1 of an account analysis statement.

Relationship Summary

The relationship summary section of analysis statements is only shown for the relationship summary account. Different analysis systems put account relationships together in a variety of ways but in the end, such a statement is designed to be a summary representation for all subsidiary accounts in the defined relationship. The sample relationship summary section shown here shows 3 (three) demand deposit accounts in a defined relationship. The summary statement here shows the details for each of the checking accounts. The intent here is always to show what part a deposit account played in the final analysis for the whole relationship.

ACCOUNT ANALYSIS RELATIONSHIP SUMMARY

Account Number	Name	Average Ledger Balance	Average Collected Balance	Earned Credit	Activity Charge
1111	Alpha Beta Industries Operating	12,716.08	12,716.08	123.83	49.69
2222	Alpha Beta Industries Payroll	11,100.47	11,100.47	78.55	49.35
3333	Alpha Beta Industries HSA Fund	11,266.51	11,266.51	109.71	49.39
	***** Relationship Summary**	**35,083.06**	**35,083.06**	**312.09**	**148.43**

It is interesting to note that back in the 1970's, very early renditions of this relationship summary section of the statement would only show what checking account numbers were included in the defined relationship. Today, some systems will allow the user to decide what columns should be shown for this summary. Best practice is to at least include the subsidiary account number, the fees that were calculated, and the earnings allowance calculated for each demand deposit account.

Balance Summary

The balance computation section of the analysis statement will take on various forms depending upon the situation at hand. The reserve requirement balance reduction is not nearly as common as it once was. The intent of this section is to show bank customers all the balances involved leading up to the average positive collected balance. The average positive collected is most often used as a basis for the earnings allowance calculations.

If an account were to draw into uncollected funds during the month, the average negative collected balance would also be shown here. In this example, the average positive and average collected balance are the same, which means this account did not draw into uncollected funds during the month. Had there been such a draw, the average negative collected balance would be shown and would have likely generated an additional service fee for the customer.

BALANCE COMPUTATION FOR THE PERIOD	
Average Net Ledger Balance	35,083.06
Less Average Daily Float	.00
Average Net Collected Balance	35,083.06
Average Positive Collected Balance	35,083.06
Less Reserve Requirement (10.0000 %)	350.83
Balance to Support Services	34,732.23

Compensation

Like other sections of the analysis statement, this section is situational. The sample below is very basic and represents a typical display for a monthly account that is paid interest on any excess available balance.

COMPENSATION INFORMATION		
ACCOUNT POSITION FOR THE PERIOD	FEE BASIS	BALANCE BASIS
Current Period Credit (10.9325 %)	312.09	34,732.23
Current Period Analyzed Charges	148.43	18,353.37
Analyzed Charges Due After Credit	.00	
Total Fees Now Due	.00	
Interest Credit (2.71%)	36.48	16,378.86

While the paper statement standard for account analysis shows balances and fees in a single column, the standard also provides for using multiple amount columns to save on space and improve readability. The display shown above for example, makes it very clear that the balance basis for the earnings allowance calculation is 34,732.23 as it is shown right next to the calculated earnings allowance.

Following strict statement standards for account analysis, the same account information would be shown on a statement with everything in a single column. Here is a sample with recommended descriptions and amount related AFP Codes (the AFP Codes are intentionally masked):

AFP Code	Description	Amount
00 00 XX	Investable Balance	34,732.23
00 04 XX	Balance Equivalent – Total Service Charge	18,353.37
00 04 XX	Excess / (Deficit) Collected Balance	16,378.86
00 02 XX	Earnings Allowance	312.09
00 03 XX	Balance Compensable Service Charges	148.43
00 02 XX	Excess / (Deficit) Earnings Allowance	163.66

This section takes on even a different look for non-monthly compensation cycle accounts. Non-monthly accounts have an accrued earnings allowance and accrued charges from previous cycles. Some systems net these two figures and carry the net forward to the following month. Best practices lean toward granularity, so accrued earnings kept separate from accrued charges supports clearer reporting each month.

Customers with a non-monthly compensation cycle still receive analysis statements monthly. These are commonly referred to as *positional* statements that reflect the current account position each month. The actual debiting of charges (if any) doesn't take place on such accounts until the compensation cycle for the account comes due. An account on an annual compensation cycle due in the month of December will get positional statements every month (all year) but only the December statement will reflect the final fees due (if any).

Service Detail

The customer analysis statement typically shows the *Service Detail* section of a statement in a very organised fashion, arranged by the product category assigned to each line-item service. The AFP Service Code is generally only used by larger banks with their commercial billing. The Bank Transaction Code (aka. BTC, Bank Service ID Code, Bank Identifier Code) is almost never shown in this section but I am showing below for illustration purposes. Having both codes in this section of the statement makes it easier for people to discuss statement issues with specific line-item services.

SERVICE INFORMATION

BANK CODE	AFP CODE	SERVICES RENDERED IN PERIOD	VOLUME	UNIT PRICE	SERVICE CHARGE	BALANCE REQUIRED
		*** Balance Based Services**				
DP111		Balance Assessment Fee	35.09	.291545	10.23	1,265
		*** Subtotal Balance Based Services**			**10.23**	**1,265**
		*** Depository Services**				
22051		DDA Statement - Paper	3	5.0000	15.00	1,855
CK049		Account Maintenance	3	10.0000	30.00	3,710
		*** Subtotal Depository Services**			**45.00**	**5,565**
		*** ACH Origination Services**				
2500	25 00 00	ACH Origination Maintenance	1	50.0000	50.00	6,182
2501	25 01 01	ACH Credits	4	.2000	.80	99
2502	25 01 00	ACH Debits	12	.2000	2.40	297
2503	25 05 01	ACH Files	4	10.0000	40.00	4,446
		*** Subtotal ACH Origination Services**			**93.20**	**11,0[illegible]**

Within each product category, few analysis systems allow for customized sequencing of services and often display line-item services in the bank's service code order on the statement (not very helpful or meaningful to a customer).

A point to be made here is that the statement sequence and placement of a service becomes a very natural expectation of where one might find or locate a service. For example, over time one might begin to learn that the *Lockbox Maintenance Fee* in account analysis is always the first service line listed in the Lockbox Product Category. Whether in the analysis system itself or on the statement, a user begins to expect that services would be (by default) in a very meaningful order and the most meaningful order of all is the statement sequence of services. There may be a situation where one wants to see the service ordering by some other data element, but the statement presentation of services is by far the most meaningful and useful to anyone.

Another point to be made is one of consistency. Whether viewing services on a statement or anywhere in an analysis system, I've always felt the services should be presented in a consistent order and style. In designing an approach to accomplish both customization and to promote consistency, I once employed the use of a statement sequence number for every line-item service definition. The design incorporated a tool to drag and drop services (and groups of services) into a user desired sequence. When the sequence was saved, all the statement sequence numbers were re-ordered and written into service definition records. Until changed again, that became the precise sequence of how services were displayed on a customer statement. The statement sequence also became the default sequence order for all services on reports, grids, selection tools, basically everywhere in the account analysis system.

Service Detail Subtotals

The AFP (Association for Financial Professionals) is the author of the AFP Service Codes. The AFP Service Codes are recognized as the industry standard for identifying service charges that appear on account analysis statements and in responding to corporate RFP's.

Today, there are more than 2,500 domestic AFP Service Codes identified by the AFP and these code assignments include *subtotal* services. Subtotal services are typically found on account analysis statements at the end of a product category / family of services. An analysis statement organised along the lines of AFP standards, would show services of like type in their various product categories.

While some analysis systems support the concept of displaying AFP codes on statements, the product category description is often more free form on such statements and may or may not be using AFP recommended product category descriptions. Subtotal services are a part of all services with assigned AFP codes.

Service Detail Summary					
AFP Code	Description	Volume	Unit Price	Service Charge	Balance Equivalent
	* ACH Origination Services				
250000	ACH Origination Module Maintenance	1	50.0000	$ 50.00	$ 325,893
250100	ACH Debits Originated	23	0.2000	$ 4.60	$ 29,982
250101	ACH Credits Originated	245	0.2000	$ 49.00	$ 319,375
	ACH Addendas Originated	4	0.2500	$ 1.00	$ 6,518
	ACH Items - Same Day Surcharge	5	1.0000	$ 5.00	$ 32,589
	ACH Returns	2	5.0000	$ 10.00	$ 65,179
	ACH Re-deposited Items	6	1.5000	$ 9.00	$ 58,661
250501	ACH Transmissions Per File	4	10.0000	$ 40.00	$ 260,714
	ACH Items Deleted	56	15.0000	$ 840.00	$ 5,475,002
	ACH Files Deleted	1	40.0000	$ 40.00	$ 260,714
	ACH Items Reversed	7	15.0000	$ 105.00	$ 684,375
	ACH Files Reversed	2	40.0000	$ 80.00	$ 521,429
	ACH Notification of Change	2	2.0000	$ 4.00	$ 26,071

The statement example above shows a list of ACH Origination services, some with their assigned AFP Service Code and a subtotal for all the services in the product family. Most AFP Service Codes are not shown as they are copyrighted material. The AFP Service Codes shown here are displayed with permission granted by the AFP.

Not all analysis systems support the display of a services *subtotal* on the statement. When shown, subtotal services highlight the total fees and balance required for each product family of services. While AFP Service Codes are not commonly displayed on analysis statements, product subtotals are commonly shown.

In one system I personally designed, I developed a technique for building these subtotal lines as a special type of service (a subtotal service). These special services were designed to be placed into the service blueprint at very specific locations where the end user wanted to see a subtotal drawn on the statement. Subtotal services also served to create separation (spacing) of the line-item services on the analysis statement and to enhance the overall appearance. While not shown here, waived services are not typically included in the product subtotals, for good reason.

Subtotal services also serve a very specific purpose when a bank is using bottom line discounting, which is a subject of its' own.

Service Detail Summary					
	Description	Volume	Unit Price	Service Charge	
	* Depository Services				
	Deposit Ticket	5	0.7500	$ 3.75	F
	Deposited Items - On Us	67	0.2000	$ 13.40	
	* Subtotal Depository Services			$ 17.15	
	Discount On Depository Services (20%)			$ (3.43)	

Service Summary

The service summary section of the account analysis statement normally follows immediately after the service detail information. This statement section is designed to summarise all the line-item services.

SERVICE SUMMARY		
Total Analyzed Charges	148.43	18,354
Total Fee Based Charges	.00	
Total Service Charges	148.43	18,354

Balance Requirement Messaging

The balance multiplier is not always seen on analysis statements, but it is provided for in the paper statement standards. The intent behind this message is to let a customer know exactly how much of a balance is needed to offset the compensable service charges on the statement, at the given earnings allowance rate. Normally, almost all service charges are compensable (A-Analyzed) so this is a very meaningful message to a customer.

$123.65 in Collected Balance will offset $1.00 of analyzed service charges.
This factor includes a provision for reserves.

Customers normally think of their checking account balance when they are trying to figure out how to have all their service charges offset. This message though, refers to the account's collected balance and even then, may stipulate the amount shown has taken the bank's reserve requirement rate into consideration.

The calculation for the balance multiplier is only affected by the earnings allowance rate (aka. ECR-Earnings Credit Rate) and whether the bank is still taking a reserve requirement from the account balance. If no reserve requirement exists, the calculation is as follows:

Balance Multiplier = $1.00 / (ECR x (Days in Period / Days in Year))

The result of this calculation will let the account holder know they will need $XXX.XX amount of average balance in their account, to offset $1.00 of calculated service charge.

Historical Performance

Ideally, the statement design would support a bar chart showing fees over the previous 12 months. Now that statements are seldom mailed, banks can include more information on their analysis statements.

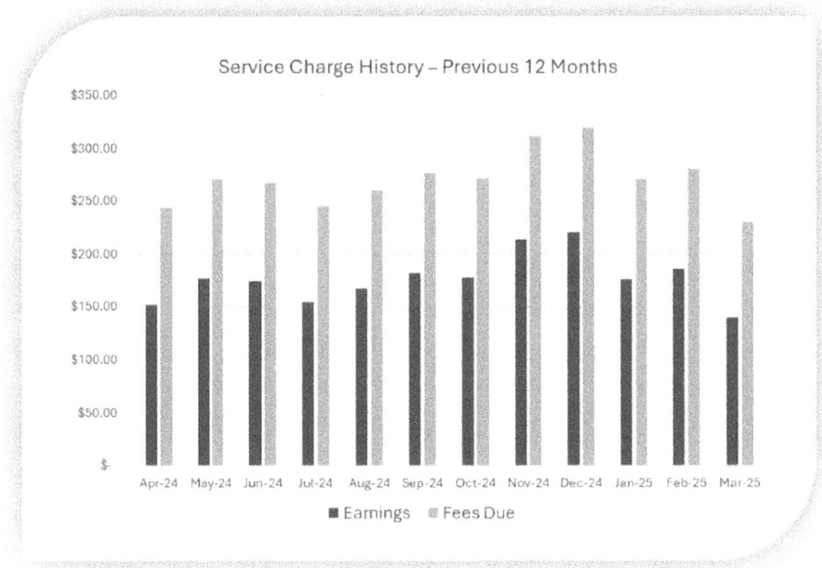

Five

Application Integrations

Because account analysis encompasses the commercial billing of all treasury management products and services, you can just imagine both the primary and ancillary systems that require integration with account analysis. There are numerous inputs to any analysis system but there are also important outputs from analysis into downstream systems such as general ledger, data warehouse, image archives, and others.

This chapter will review what data is fed into the account analysis system and where this data is obtained from. The chapter will also cover the most common outputs of commercial billing needed for downstream systems. While most inputs and outputs to this point in history have been based on batch file integrations, I will also cover the integration of CRM systems with account analysis, which have been more prevalent of late, along with the use of APIs to connect with external systems.

Integration with the Core Deposit System

The core deposit system is the primary source of account information when it comes to account analysis and commercial billing. The core deposit system is typically the system of record for all accounts on commercial analysis and as such, the accounts' name & address, demographic information, and balances are all obtained from the core DDA system. Some core DDA systems (not all) will pass information to the analysis system daily keeping the analysis system in synchronisation with the core.

Analysis systems use the name & address for statements (although few are still being mailed). The account demographic information passed to analysis allows the analysis system to organise reporting by branch, cost center, account type, etc. The analysis system uses the daily balances to formulate average balances for the month. Uncollected funds fees are commonly created for any day where a draw into uncollected funds is discovered. The daily balances help analysis systems understand the minimum balances for the month too, which are sometimes used in the control of pricing.

Volumes and counts are also passed from the core deposit system to the analysis system. These counts are used to assess service fees for the month. The deposit system normally passes counts for depository services like checks, deposits, and deposited items. The core system interface might also send counts for ACH, Wires, and more. Best practice is to use the best possible source for data when it comes to commercial billing.

Conversion Only Considerations

There are very specific data items needed at conversion time when setting up a new analysis system. The interface to the core deposit system will make sure accounts are added to analysis and kept up to date daily but there are a few data elements that will likely be needed from the existing analysis system as one prepares for conversion to a new one. The list of specific data points needed for conversion are as follows:

- -Relationship Parent Account Number (Controls linkage)
- -Account Specific Earnings Allowance / Interest Rate

- -Account Settlement Option (Invoice, Auto Debit, etc.)
- -Account Waive Option (Billing Code)
- -Account Compensation Cycle (Frequency; Quarterly, etc.)
- -Account Exception Service Pricing (by Service Code)
- -Account Specific Recurring Fees (by Service Code)

Even with a core deposit system integration in place, the above data elements need to be handled during a conversion to a new account analysis system. During normal monthly operation, these listed items are set up using the user interface of the new analysis system. If the existing system has 200 accounts for example, who are being billed via Invoice, those accounts need special handling in the conversion process to ensure they are all set up correctly. For any such mass changes, an ETL-Extract, Translate, and Load process is often used to ensure all exceptions are set up properly.

Service Billing Files

Overview

When it comes to integrating data into the commercial billing system, what is most talked about is not the core deposit system information but instead, it is the service billing file charges and counts from ancillary systems. Even a small bank will have numerous treasury management products that need to be involved with the customer billing process. Any account analysis implementation will involve numerous service billing files but what is needed from each file is the same basic information.

Data Content

Service billing files are used to bill deposit accounts for their usage of each treasury product. Essential to any service billing file is an account number. The account number will be used to pass service counts too. Unless every record on a service billing file is for the exact same service, the file will typically contain a service code to delineate what the stated volume is (e.g. an outgoing wire or an incoming wire). Service codes are typically mapped out in the account analysis system, so the system understands each volume passed. Service billing files will certainly have a volume (or charge) attached to each record as well.

Some analysis systems will call for an effective date of a service record, but account analysis is essentially a monthly billing system so the actual effective date of a particular volume (as in the case of a Wire Transfer), is not terribly important to the billing process. Essentially then, think of a service billing file as a file where each record provides an account number, a service code, and a volume / charge for each service.

A bank running an account analysis system will likely have many service billing files because they come from many different parts of the bank. While very limited data is needed from each file, the service billing files typically contain numerous data elements. Many service billing files are originated by third- party vendors. The complexity of processing service billing files stems from each service billing file being so different, not from the actual data elements needed from each file.

Account analysis vendors have gone out of their way to make processing service billing files as easy as possible. Data mapping and conversion tools have been developed over time so given meta-data, a vendor's billing file can be consumed by the analysis system without much programming. Still, there are new files created with every new treasury management vendor so the battle for simplicity and speed to revenue in handling service billing files rages on.

Service Billing Data Lacking Automation

When approached by any third-party vendor to solicit products and services, the first question of any banker should be "do you have an automated billing file so we can charge our accounts for use of your service?". Vendors don't always realize that banks need the ability to pass charges on to those accounts using external services. Still today, we have service providers such as armored car services, sending invoices to the bank with the expectation the invoices will be paid (in real dollars).

The invoices from armored car services for example, will often be very detailed showing every business of the bank that was provided such services. These invoices can often be lengthy and consist of several pages. Some banks will go through the painful process of looking up deposit account numbers and entering this billing data into the account analysis system. Others will toss the invoice aside due to the overwhelming manual data entry required to pass those fees through.

In more than one implementation of a commercial billing system, I had banks request a PDF copy of an invoice (or scan a paper invoice to create a PDF). With the advancement of OCR-Optical Character Recognition, there are now tools available to automatically convert PDFs to MS Excel files. While MS Excel will be a digital version of the invoices, the data still needs formatting, and some will use a cut and paste approach, which is still better than manual data entry. Over the years, I've become adept at creating macros in visual basic, to basically scrape these MS Excel versions of invoices. The scraping process would extract the customer's name and then look up the "using account number" for billing. As long as an invoice has some consistent pattern to it, scraping the data with macros is very effective in the creation of formatted billing data for upload into the billing system.

> *In a real-world situation, a banker's bank was getting an 87-page invoice from a vendor that did shredding for member banks (as a service). The account analysis operations team was struggling with the invoice from the shredding company every month, so we converted the PDF to MS Excel (using an OCR-Optical Character Recognition tool) and I wrote a macro to scrape the Excel worksheet. The customer names were converted to billing account numbers automatically (via the macro) with the translations stored in a secondary worksheet of the macro. The line-item charges were all scraped / extracted, and the amounts were all surcharged by 5% before passing on to the analysis system. Upon completion of the automated process (which took a few human steps and maybe 10 minutes), you should have seen the expression on the face of the person who was looking up account numbers and keying this invoice into account analysis every month! Where there is a will, there is always a way.*

Data Warehouse

Not everyone thinks about the data warehouse when the subject turns to account analysis. I love telling the story of doing an implementation for a new commercial billing system at a large regional bank in Texas. The bank created all their management reporting from their internal data warehouse. Any new system being installed at the bank was required to feed the bank's data warehouse with the appropriate information / data points. Sometimes feeding a data warehouse will mean custom development as was the case in my situation.

The beauty of the approach though, was that even though the bank moved to a new commercial billing system, internal bank management didn't have to decipher any new reporting. The bank literally implemented an entirely new account analysis system, but the monthly reporting on product revenue, profitability, fee income, etc. hadn't changed at all. The bank's data warehouse was fed daily with anything that changed in account analysis (pricing, adjustments, re-analyzed statements, etc.).

Feeding the data warehouse can be a challenge depending upon what data is going to be populated there for all to see. It seems all banks share the monthly statement data which amounts to one row / record of data (demographics, balances, total fees, etc.) for each account on analysis. The statement data also includes line-item service fees where multiple rows / records are sent to the data warehouse for each account. The best approach for feeding a data warehouse is to supply all the necessary data for an account analysis statement to be reproduced if needed. The account analysis statement is not typically reproduced in data warehouse reporting, but the data is all there, so any reporting one would require from account analysis is available. I think of the data warehouse as a raw data repository while an image archive (commonly accessed by online banking systems) would contain the actual images of account analysis statements.

Beyond account analysis statement information for each month, a data warehouse might also contain all the current pricing data for treasury management products and services. CRM systems often want to obtain current pricing data and the bank's data warehouse is a great repository for such. The data warehouse can also serve as a pricing history data store for looking back in time at service pricing.

General Ledger

In many instances, general ledger entries of significance for account analysis are taken care of by the core deposit system. In other words, if debits / credits are passed to the DDA system and processed there, the debit / credit totals are often accounted for by the DDA system passing transaction totals to the general ledger system. Still, some analysis systems will create general ledger entries and feed them to the bank's G/L system. This is especially true when a bank does invoice billing for customers where the accounts receivable entries need to be made to the G/ L.

There are a variety of general ledger system vendors in the industry, no two systems are the same. Some G/L systems have reporting embedded within that banks often want to take advantage of. This is especially true when a bank is unable to obtain certain reports from the account analysis system itself. Similar to using an internal data warehouse for reporting, a G/L system can be set up with contra accounts for account analysis reporting. As long as the analysis system passes the appropriate information to G/L, a bank will be able to take advantage of the G/L system reporting capabilities.

For example, most G/L systems need to know total fees debited, total interest credited, and any accounts receivable amounts to be posted. This same information is often provided to G/L by account analysis broken down by cost center, enabling the G/L system to report on these accounting entries by cost center.

In rare cases, I have been asked to provide gross revenue by service code within a cost center. Any time a G/L requirement involving gross revenue pops up, you can be sure the request surrounds reporting within the G/L system. G/L is primarily focused on actual changes to balances in the bank, changes created by fee debits and interest credits. When a requirement defines gross revenue as being needed, it is typically for informational purposes only (a contra account in G/L). Requests for gross revenue by service code or product family are often combined with requests for total earnings allowance and earnings allowance used to cover fees. These figures are all needed to arrive at net debits/credits for the G/L.

Another reason a bank may want to use the G/L system for reporting is simply user access. If a bank has finance employees accessing the G/L system for reporting already, there typically isn't much desire to now have these same users go into yet another system for essentially the same information.

The best practice is to have the account analysis system provide all such reporting as it is the system of record for manufacturing all the numbers in the first place. When the account analysis system is unable to provide such reporting, feeding a G/L system with monthly details so that the reporting tool within G/L system can be used by finance, is a clever alternative.

CRM Systems

Banks are constantly trying to improve the tools being used by their treasury management salespeople. The software tools developed over the years have provided treasury salespeople with improved methods of keeping track of their sales opportunities. These sales opportunities involve new treasury products for existing customers and new customers altogether. Managing all the opportunities can be a challenge without an advanced CRM – Customer Relationship Management system.

When it comes to commercial billing, CRM systems primarily need to know the products and services being offered by the bank and even more important is the pricing that goes along with all the products and services. Without a separate CRM system, a bank could provide salespeople access to the account analysis system but if the bank has invested in a centralized CRM system, they most often would want all salespeople to use that single system and not have access to additional resources like account analysis.

When integration with a CRM system is required, there are a few touchpoints where the account analysis system needs to work hand in hand with the CRM system. The best practice would be to use API calls back and forth between account analysis and the CRM system. Lacking API's, I typically see file integration between CRM and account analysis but regardless of integration method, CRM systems typically want to know the following:

- -What Products and Services are available to potential treasury management customers?
- -What is the current pricing for the services being proposed?
- -What accounts are in the current customer portfolio?
- -How are the customer's accounts related to one another?
- -What products and/or Services does a customer already use?

When CRM systems activate a product or service for a customer, there is often an automated touch point where certain fees can be set up in account analysis via CRM. A monthly recurring maintenance fee, for example, might be something set up automatically by CRM when a new product is sold. This approach helps to reduce errors in onboarding accounts.

Some CRM integrations may also create the necessary transactions to apply special pricing to services in account analysis. This way, an exception price for an account can automatically be applied without further manual intervention.

More advanced CRM systems have account modeling capabilities embedded within, so a customer proposal can flow through a value-based approval workflow before getting to account analysis. Integrating account analysis with external modeling systems like this can be a bit more challenging because this often involves numerous settings, such as account relationship settings, exception pricing for services, recurring fees for specific products, etc. It also means not integrating any of such until the proper approvals are complete.

As APIs become more prevalent throughout the industry, communication between CRM systems and account analysis systems are certain to improve. Adding accounts, setting up products, establishing special pricing, etc. will all become API calls from one system to another. The best practice for an account analysis vendor would be to provide these APIs and thus provide the conduit needed for straight through processing.

PART II: Banking Roles & Best Practices

My experience has been that commercial account analysis affects many departments within a bank, and each department is very focused on different aspects of what the account analysis system produces. The finance department for example is very interested in the accounting for every product and service. Sales and marketing are constantly coming up with new ideation for advertising and selling the treasury management services for the bank. While most look at account analysis purely as a billing system, it truly is a treasury management service of its own in that it provides commercial customers with an earnings allowance.

In addition to roles and best practices, this part of the account analysis guide will address management reporting and the role it plays in commercial billing. Vendor software systems have all sorts of reporting within them today, but here I take the approach of describing actionable data views that one could and should produce from any account analysis database or data warehouse, if it is not already provided.

What you will find in the chapters that follow are a collection of ideas, practices, and perhaps unique services that banks have put into place over the years, using their account analysis system as a driving force behind the ideation.

Six

Marketing

Marketing – The Concept of Differentiation

One doesn't often think of marketing when it comes to account analysis, but the truth is, a bank has a tremendous opportunity to win new business through the development of new products and services they offer to their commercial customers. The odds of winning greater wallet share in the market sometimes have to do with differentiation of like services from other financial institutions. If a bank can differentiate their offerings from other FI's, they have a chance to win new business on that basis alone. Simply said, a financial institution can win new business by differentiating themselves from surrounding competitors.

Having implemented analysis systems at so many banks, I found myself saying sometimes, "okay, now I have seen it all", only to find that phrase was not true at all. Following you will find distinct subject areas very specific to commercial account analysis, where various system features allowed banks to create differentiation for themselves, in a focused effort to win new business.

Balance Directed Pricing

One powerful but not often seen approach to pricing is the concept of *Balance Directed Pricing*. One reason this is not often seen is because there are very few commercial account analysis systems able to accommodate such an approach.

A feature like *Balance Directed Pricing* can be very helpful in the development of a new approach to winning new business. In an environment where ECR's (Earnings Credit Rates) are very low, it can be very costly to try and win new business simply by offering higher ECR's. High ECR's result in earnings allowances that are applied across all treasury management products and services in total. A feature like *Balance Directed Pricing* allows one to focus on a single (perhaps most profitable) product / service vs. giving away the *farm* in the form of higher ECR's.

Balance Range	AFP Code	Service	Unit Price	For Volume
Average Collected Balance Up To $100,000	350202	Outgoing Domestic Wires	Free	Up To 5
			$25.00	Up to 10
			$20.00	Over 10
Average Collected Balance Over $100,000 Up To $500,000			Free	Up To 10
	350202	Outgoing Domestic Wires	$25.00	Up to 20
			$20.00	Over 20
Average Collected Balance Over $500,000	350202	Outgoing Domestic Wires	Free	Up To 20
			$25.00	Up to 30
			$20.00	Over 30

It is a very simple concept really, the higher a customer's balance goes up, the cheaper the treasury services become. A technique like this motivates the behavior of keeping higher balances on deposit, if only to reduce bank fees.

If your commercial billing system has the capability of controlling pricing in this manner and your competition is unable to provide such a feature (even if they wanted to) one could clearly gain a competitive edge by simply implementing a *Balance Directed Pricing* approach.

Rolling Over Excess Earnings

Few commercial billing systems have the capability of Rolling Over Excess Earnings Allowance from one month to the next, for accounts using a monthly compensation cycle. As a result, very few banks would even think of doing so. Systems that come close to providing roll over functionality typically do not have limit controls in place. Without minimum/maximum limit controls, using a roll over strategy can get out of control.

Many billing systems support the concept of non-monthly compensation cycles where customers settle fees quarterly, semi-annually, annually, etc. Non-monthly compensation cycles are common in the industry though and simply delay (or put off) the charging of an account. Using non-monthly cycles is not very helpful in gaining a competitive edge though, because most banks could do this with their analysis system.

Rolling Over Excess Earnings Allowance can be very helpful in the development of a new approach to winning new business. It is a very simple concept really, if a customer who is normally billed monthly ends up in an *excess* balance position for the month, the earnings allowance represented by the excess position is carried forward into the next billing cycle. Any excess earnings allowance below a minimum, or above a maximum, would be thrown out and forgotten (as is done with the entire excess allowance when there is no rollover strategy).

Balance Summary	
Average Ledger Balance	$ 598,198.12
Less Average Float	$ 182,364.00
Average Collected Balance	$ 415,834.12
Less Reserve Requirement (10%)	$ 41,583.41
Investable Balance	$ 374,250.71
Less Balance Required for Services	$ 213,343.36
Excess (Deficit) Balance	$ 160,917.35

Results Summary	
Earnings Credit at .50% of Investable Balance	$158.92
Less Total Analyzed Fees	$ 90.59
Net Analyzed Result	$ 68.33

The sample shown here has an excess allowance of $68.33. If your bank allowed a rollover of excess earnings capped at $50, this customer would enjoy a $50 earnings credit heading into the next month of billing.

If an account analysis system has the capability of rolling over excess earnings each month and bank competition is unable to provide such a feature, one could gain a competitive edge simply by *Rolling Over Excess Earnings Allowance.*

Rolling Compensation Cycles

The compensation cycle for bank customers represents a rather significant point in an accounts service charge lifecycle. Most customers in account analysis have a monthly compensation cycle and as it turns out, this is most advantageous to the bank. A monthly compensation cycle means the account service charges will be calculated at the end of each month and if they are greater than the calculated earnings allowance for the month, the difference will most commonly be auto debited from the customer's designated deposit account.

As one might imagine, a quarterly or annual compensation cycle works in the same way but the decision making on a service charge encompasses the accrued charges and accrued earnings over more months, before the line in the sand is drawn. Most account analysis solutions in the industry support the concept of monthly compensation cycles and non-monthly compensation cycles. The non-monthly compensation cycles are more favorable to a bank's customer because more months of data are aggregated before a charge / no charge decision is made based upon the earnings allowance being enough to cover all charges. When service charges exceed earnings for any given period, an account is known to be in a deficit position.

For non-monthly compensation cycle accounts, analysis statements normally are still produced monthly so customers understand the position they are currently in along the way (excess of deficit).

A feature not often seen in account analysis systems is something referred to as *rolling* compensation cycles. Rolling compensation cycles evolved from banks losing out on accounts having a non-monthly compensation cycle in the first place (of course banks could simply adopt a policy of not allowing non-monthly cycles but that subject falls under policy making, not marketing).

Assuming a bank allows an annual compensation cycle for example, an account will accrue charges and earnings over an entire year (some systems allow one to specify the month, so it doesn't have to be December). At the end of the year, the system will make the determination on whether an account is in an excess position or a deficit position and charge accordingly.

An annual rolling compensation cycle works a bit differently. Once a year begins, the system will look for the excess/deficit position at the end of the month. The system will consider the current month (and up to the previous 11 months) if an account has never been charged. If the result of the calculation finds an account in a deficit position, the account is charged and then the year starts over again. If the account is in an excess position, nothing will happen, and the account's earnings and charges are rolled forward.

Using this rolling cycle approach, an account could be in a deficit position each month where a service charge would be debited, and the account is continually starting over. An account could also be in an excess position each month where continually, nothing happens. Keep in mind though, that an annual rolling cycle will limit the review to only 12 months (the current month and up to the previous 11 months).

Where a compensation cycle line has been drawn in the sand, the calculations always stop short of including a month where a charge was already taken. Any time a charge is taken, an account starts the rolling compensation cycle over again.

> *“A $14b dollar bank in southern California once decided that all accounts on analysis will have a rolling compensation cycle. This was attractive to customers vs. settling fees every month by default. The rolling cycle gave customers a chance to have more in earnings allowance next month. This marketing approach was attractive to the bank because they could offer treasury management customers a billing program never heard of at other banks. The truth is that the account analysis system used at some of the other banks didn't have the capability of calculating fees for rolling compensation cycles. The $14b dollar bank in this case had a competitive edge over the other banks in the area.”*

Handling Complex Billing Relationships

Having the capability to handle any of the complexities surrounding settlement and billing for large commercial banking relationships can make all the difference a bank needs to win new business. Many commercial billing solutions support the concept of demand deposit accounts being linked together to form a relationship summary of accounts. Few if any billing solutions support the concept of relationship summaries becoming subsidiary to higher level summaries (spanning multiple levels) with actual settlement of bank fees happening at any desired level within the structure.

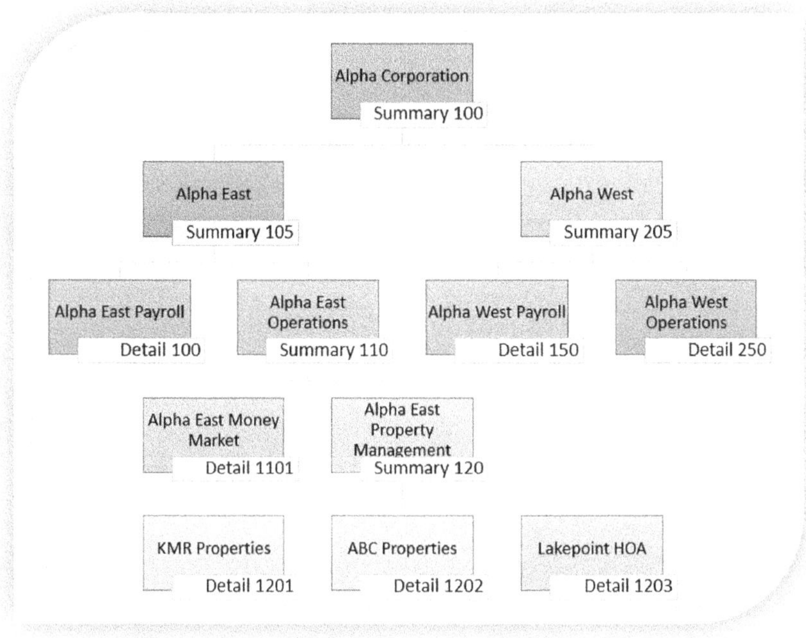

A billing diagram for the Alpha Corporation is shown above. Imagine a financial institution being able to systematically handle the billing for a relationship with this complexity. The actual charging of bank fees could be needed for any one of the levels shown. While all fees should roll up to *Alpha Corporation Summary 100*, for reporting purposes the actual debiting for portions of the total fees may be needed at selected levels".

Sometimes different types of fees need to be charged at different levels. Selected property management services for example, may need to be auto charged for accounts 1201 – 1203, while all other services for these same detail accounts may need to roll up for summary account analysis (and earnings credit offset).

If a bank's commercial billing system has the capability of handling complex relationship structures such as this and the bank's competition is unable to provide such functionality, one could clearly gain a competitive edge. Handling Complex Billing Relationships like this will also earn a heightened reputation for a bank, simply for the ability to do so.

Minimum Fees For Services

Having the capability to handle any of the complexities surrounding settlement and billing for large commercial banking relationships, can make quite a difference in winning new business.

All commercial billing solutions support the concept of applying a unit price to a volume resulting in a charge (even if the unit pricing structure is tiered). More advanced billing solutions support the concept of a M*inimum Fee* being applied to the *Price * Volume* calculation. A minimum fee for a particular service is perhaps one of the easiest negotiations to have when it comes to bank fees. A business customer will always be seeking a lower price and will probably be promising volumes that may or may not be achievable (or sustainable). The perfect middle ground can be a concession price for a service with a minimum monthly fee guarantee.

> *If a client suggests they'll have approximately 30 items a month for a particular service, allowing a concession price with a minimum charge can reduce the risk of revenue opportunity lost.*

If a bank's commercial billing system has the capability of handling minimum fees for each/any service being offered, one could possibly afford to offer lower unit pricing for select services giving the bank a competitive advantage. The optics of lower unit pricing can win new business for a bank. Perhaps the greatest benefit of a minimum fee capability is simply the ability to use this pricing feature in the negotiation process. If one has this feature / capability in the billing system and the competition across the street does not, a bank will have gained a competitive edge in pricing.

Bottom Line Discounting

Discounting fees in account analysis can be accomplished by either reducing the unit price of line-item services or by leaving the standard unit prices (aka. list prices) as they are and show separate statement lines that highlight any *reduction* in fees calculated. In either case discounts are calculated before any taxes on service charges.

Some analysis systems take the approach of automating a reduction in unit prices by a percentage rate (whether it be for specific product categories or an entire account). A disadvantage to unit price discounting is that it forces an institution to provide percentage discounts *before* the earnings allowance is applied because all line-item service calculations are computed before any earnings credit is applied.

Manipulating unit pricing to achieve discounts has a disadvantage in that the amount of the savings is not clear to the customer on the analysis statement. An analysis system might highlight that a unit price is NOT standard, but the analysis statement doesn't make clear just how much money was saved by the discount, the statement simply shows a unit price that is lower than the list price for a specific service.

I once designed a discount approach where the analysis system was more focused on separate statement lines showing a reduction in fees vs. altering service unit prices. Separate discount lines could even be used for an entire category of services, or at the account level (for total fee-based and/or compensable services). At one bank where this approach was implemented, it was referred to as *Bottom Line Discounting*. Showing separate line(s) for the discounts highlights the fee savings on analysis statements for bank customers.

When one considers applying a % discount at the product category or account level, showing the fee savings makes perfect sense and can create customer loyalty. The following sample shows a customer that has been set up with a 10% discount on analysed charges and a 10% discount on fee-based charges too.

ACCOUNT POSITION FOR THE PERIOD	FEE BASIS	BALANCE BASIS
Current Period Credit (0.5000 %)	$55.48	$150,000.00
Current Period Analyzed Charges	$152.97	$413,585.56
Analyzed Charges Due after Credit	$97.49	
Less Discount on Analyzed Fees (10%)	(9.75)	
Plus Fee-Based Charges in Period	$3.75	
Less Fee Based Charges Discount (10%)	(0.38)	
Fees Debited to Your Account	$91.11	
Balance Shortage for the Current Period		(263,585.56)

The analysed charge discount above is *after* earnings credit. The discount is rounded up to 9.75 from 9.749. Such discounts offered after earnings credit cost the bank **less** than the likes of discounts *before* earnings credit. All unit price discounts are before earnings credit in account analysis because earnings credits are only applied to the total compensable charges.

In the sample below, the exact same results are shown with a 10% discount on analysed charges before earnings credit. This sample below is very similar to results obtained by altering all the unit prices by 10%.

ACCOUNT POSITION FOR THE PERIOD	FEE BASIS	BALANCE BASIS
Current Period Credit (0.5000 %)	$55.48	$150,000.00
Current Period Analyzed Charges	$152.97	$413,585.56
Analyzed Charges Due after Credit	$97.49	
Less Discount on Analyzed Fees (10%)	(15.30)	
Plus Fee-Based Charges in Period	$3.75	
Less Fee Based Charges Discount (10%)	(0.38)	
Fees Debited to Your Account	$85.56	
Balance Shortage for the Current Period		(263,585.56)

When applying the 10% discount to the analysed fees <u>before</u> earnings credit, the calculated discount to fees due (15.30) when compared to analysed fees that would have been due without any discount (97.49) turns out to be larger than 10% (15.30 / 97.49 = almost 16%).

From a marketing perspective, using the analysed fees due before credit to calculate discounts will show a discount for all accounts with any fees calculated at all. Using the after-credit option when doing the calculation only will show a discount when an account is in a deficit position and has fees that are due. While perhaps better for marketing, the before credit option clearly is more costly to the bank.

Discounts that encompass the entire account include all fees calculated for the account regardless of which services / product families are being used by the account. Product family level discounts (another form of bottom-line discounts) involve a reduction in fees based upon the total fees calculated for the entire product family of services.

An approach I once designed for discounting before credit involved a special type of line-item service called a *discount* service. Technically, a discount service could be placed anywhere in the sequence of services on an analysis statement, but they typically would be placed right after product family sub-totals to generate discounts for the entire product family.

Service Detail Summary

Description	Volume	Unit Price	Service Charge	
* **Depository Services**				
Deposit Ticket	5	0.7500	3.75	F
Deposited Items - On Us	67	0.2000	13.40	
* **Subtotal Depository Services**			17.15	
Discount On Depository Services (20%)			(3.43)	
* **Disbursement Services**				
Checks Paid	158	0.2000	31.60	
Returned Items	10	10.0000	100.00	
* **Subtotal Disbursement Services**			131.60	
Discount On Disbursement Services (10%)			(13.16)	

Notice in the illustration above, a 10% discount has been placed on the disbursement services product family. The discount service is typically on the standard price list with a 0% rate but then for any account or price list, the rate can be set to some value (e.g. -10%). The discount service in this context is designed to compute a discount value based upon the charge amount in the previous line item on the statement. When placed after a product family sub-total, the discount becomes a percentage of all fees in the product family. If the discount service was placed after the *Return Item(s)* charge of 100.00, the discount line would have been for -$10.00 vs. -$13.16.

With some analysis systems, discounting is completely focused on the automated internal reduction of unit prices (either for all services on the account or a specific product group). *Bottom Line Discounting* in general is completely focused on calculated results (either for the entire account or for a product group). Technically, both methods of discounting could co-exist even though it wouldn't be practical to reduce all unit prices by 10% and then take 10% off the bottom line for fees due as well.

Discounts after credit are less costly to a bank. When applied after earnings allowance at the account level, a 10% discount really is a 10% discount and costs the bank less than any discount calculated before earnings credit. Another distinct advantage to bottom line discounting is the display on the account analysis statement. The analysis statements clearly show how much of a savings is being attained via the discounts, thus creating customer loyalty.

It is technically possible to have a single service with a discounted unit price, a percentage discount on the product family where the service resides, and an account level discount on the entire account. All these settings (while impractical) could co-exist in some systems and would absolutely reduce overall fees.

Some banks have gone to the effort of calculating the dollar amount of fees that would have been due had such discounting not been present. This calculation allows a summary message on the analysis statement such as:

You have saved 38.4% on your banking fees this month!

Excess Allowance To Cover Customer Expenses

Imagine doing business with someone who tells you they want to pay your bills for you. This is exactly what happens with some banks who have taken a rather drastic approach to what is known as hybrid account analysis.

Hybrid account analysis has become a rather common term now for banks who pay interest on a business account's excess available balance. With *Hybrid* analysis, the best practice is to use the earnings credit rate to calculate an earnings allowance covering the customer's treasury management fees at the bank. Once the compensable bank fees are all covered, interest is calculated on the excess available balance using a separate interest rate. The interest amount is paid to the customer. The term *hybrid* morphed from the account analysis process doing two different things, first covering the treasury management fees with the bank and then paying interest to the customer.

With hybrid analysis, it is the paying interest process that creates some downstream considerations, like 1099 reporting for the bank. This is normally covered by the analysis system sending the core deposit system an interest credit transaction code for any such payment, making the core deposit system responsible for year-end tax reporting for the customer (not the analysis system). Hybrid analysis has a bit of a downside in that the customer being paid interest, now will pay income taxes on that interest payment.

Through time, creative minds have come up with the idea of not actually paying that interest to the customer when the account is in an *excess* position (the available balance on hand is more than needed to cover compensable charges). Instead of paying interest to the customer, the bank informs the customer after a preliminary analysis each month that the customer is in an *excess position* and therefore, the bank is willing to pay some expenses / bills for the customer, even process the payments for the customer. In other words, paying some of a customer's invoices to cover some of their business expenses. Now you will not see this widely advertised by banks and there may be some legal guardrails around this service, but what a service! Imagine a treasury management salesperson telling a business that any excess earnings allowance each month can be used to pay bills for them.

The accounting behind this approach is rather straight forward but the process is a bit manual. The excess earnings amount is usually communicated to the customer who then sends the bank unpaid invoices they want taken care of. The bank pays those bills on behalf of their customers and then enters each invoice amount as an *analyzed* charge into their account analysis system, with each payment becoming a charge in analysis, which reduces the excess available balance. This is normally done before final analysis. The process repeats itself as needed, until any/all excess available funds are exhausted for the customer. Some analysis systems will allow the charges to be entered with a description (or addenda) so that the analysis statement will show the business customer which of their expenses have been taken care of by the bank.

This practice started in account analysis long before the Dodd Frank Reform Act which made it legal for banks to pay interest to business customers. I specifically remember seeing this practice for the first time with property management companies in California. I am not an attorney and therefore cannot comment on the entire legality of this business practice.

I will tell you though, that there are banks paying bills for their business customers thanks to account analysis. Only in account analysis do we see the calculated excess available earnings allowance. It is this excess allowance that is normally paid by interest with hybrid analysis, but in this case is instead used to pay bills for the banking customer. Because it is never actually paid to the customer, there is no interest credit payment, no 1099 reporting, and no additional taxable income reported to the business customer.

Seven

Finance & Accounting

The finance and accounting department plays an important role in account analysis & billing because this department deals with all *results* of the analysis. The results include customers who have their fees waived, automatically debited, invoiced, and in some cases, even referred to a treasury sales officer for further review.

While best practice is to have all fees automatically debited in the deposit system (creating immediate fee income), most banks have at least a few customers that are billed via invoice. An invoice from account analysis creates an increase in the accounts receivable within the bank's general ledger so it must be dealt with regardless of how many customers are billed in this manner.

Not all account analysis system vendors provide support for the concept of billing customers via invoicing. When a customer demands invoicing for the payment of bank fees, such a request creates arduous tasks for a bank's treasury management billing team willing to tackle invoicing. It certainly doesn't help banks when bank *fee monitoring* consulting firms coach corporate treasury departments to ask for an invoice of their bank fees (allowing the customer to simply not pay for something they feel is wrong).

All revenue from treasury management billing is considered non-interest income for the bank and an important part of bank profitability overall, especially in times of high interest rates when revenue from loan interest may not be doing so well.

> *While we don't often see employment positions within a bank titled "Vice President of Account Analysis", it is common to see such for "Revenue Management". In 2018, a large commercial bank in southern California did post a job opportunity online for "Vice President of Revenue Management & Account Analysis".*

Aside from dealing with all the results of account analysis, finance and accounting get involved with the pricing for products & services. Treasury Management Services normally go through re-pricing events as well and if a bank is following the best practices, the re-pricing involves an impact review and approval process. The impact reviews involve product management for service line-item or product category impact, but customer impact is also looked at closely by relationship managers. I have the opinion that the best re-pricing events involve several services being re-priced in small increments, done in such a way as to not create too much impact on any one customer.

Other departments within the bank (sales, operations, etc.) will often look to finance & accounting professionals to come up with ideation around increasing revenue and profitability for the bank, without necessarily increasing bank pricing.

Calculating Profitability In Account Analysis

There are profitability systems in the financial services industry that are used by FI's to measure the financial value of all banking customers.

Still, within account analysis there has long been an appetite for using pure commercial billing data to calculate profitability for each treasury management account / customer on analysis (perceived to be the elite banking portfolio). I believe the desire for profitability information from analysis was born back in the days of high earnings allowance rates, when bank fees were sometimes entirely covered by account balances. Without actual fees being paid, banks would struggle to understand who their best customers were.

With a calculated profitability value for each account and customer, reporting that includes ranking, trending, charting, and exporting all become possible and can be used in negotiating customer pricing, or as I like to say, "who should the bank be taking out for a round of golf vs. who should we be removing waivers from?".

> *Best practice is to store profitability values and percentages in the account analysis system database records to ease standard reporting and user's ad-hoc reporting that occurs after each month is closed. Unfortunately, few systems store this information for easy access later.*

Service Line-Item Level Profitability

Measuring account profitability in account analysis begins at the lowest level of detail, the single service line item. Each line-item service is given a cost factor which is used to calculate the expense for the service. In simple terms then, revenue minus expense would equal marginal profit.

For volume-based services in account analysis, the service expense is the actual service volume * the per/unit cost factor. For services that contain only a charge (no volume, aka. flat charge or prepriced services), the service expense is expressed as a percentage of the charge.

For example, a flat fee courier service might be $15.27 this month but the unit cost is expressed as 75% of the charge (so the actual calculated service expense would be 11.45). These types of services are often passed through by 3rd party service providers. Passed through in this context means a charge to the bank is paid by the bank and then simply passed on as is, to the bank's customer. In these cases, the cost factors are expressed as being 100% of the charge. Some analysis systems would allow a bank to surcharge for flat fees being passed through. In these cases, the cost factors may have to be adjusted for any service surcharge amount.

To calculate service line-item level profitability then, all one needs is the actual charge and the actual expense for a single service:

-Actual Service Charge $ Less Calculated Service Expense $ = Service Level Profitability $

-(Actual Service Charge $ Less Calculated Service Expense $) / Actual Service Charge = Service Level Profitability %

An example of service line-item level profitability is shown in the illustration below where the charge is $20.00 and the expense for the service is $16.00.

Treasury Management Service Calculations – P * V

Product Group	***Service Code***	***Unit Volume***	***List Price***	***Charge***
ACH	2504	4	$5.00	$20.00

Product Group	***Service Code***	***Unit Volume***	***Unit Cost***	***Expense***
ACH	2504	4	$4.00	$16.00

The dollar value of the overall service margin in this example is $4.00 and on its' own, calculates to be a 20% margin for the service.

Treasury Management Service Calculations - Margin

Product Group	***Service Code***	***Charge***	***Less Expense***	=	***Service Margin $***	***%***
ACH	2504	$20.00	$16.00		$4.00	20%

This 20% margin can quickly turn to a LOSS with concession pricing.

A service margin can change very quickly in account analysis if concession pricing is active for a service. In the illustration below, there is a concession price of $3.00 per / ACH Item vs. a price of $5.00. The expense / cost in this case didn't change at all, only the revenue from the service was changed.

Given this concession pricing, we find ourselves with a 33.3% loss instead of a 20% marginal profit.

Treasury Management Service Calculations – Concession Pricing

Product Group	*Service Code*	*Unit Volume*	*Concession Price*	*Charge*
ACH	2504	4	$3.00	$12.00

The Expense didn't change, only the Charge did.

Product Group	*Service Code*	*Unit Volume*	*Unit Cost*	*Expense*	*Service Margin $*	*%*
ACH	2504	4	$4.00	$16.00	($4.00)	(33.3%)

Marginal profitability then can be determined for every deposit account on the account analysis system. The analysis system simply needs to aggregate the charge and expense of every service line item involved in the analysis to formulate the marginal profitability of the account.

Some account analysis systems provide additional profitability measures using indirect costs for an entire product family and/or yields on demand deposit account balances (aka. FTP - Funds Transfer Pricing).

Indirect Costs By Product Category

Indirect costs cannot be attributed to any single service in analysis. Instead, indirect costs (when used at all) are calculated based upon the total revenue of all line-item services within a specific product family and then added into the total expense for an account. The indirect costs in effect reduce account level profitability but are not considered in marginal profitability of individual service line-items.

For example, if the product category *ACH Origination* consisted of 10 line-item services for an account and the line-items added up to $100.00 in charges (revenue) along with $80.00 in expense, the total of $100.00 would become the basis for an indirect cost calculation. If the bank set up an additional indirect cost of 5% for *ACH Origination*, the analysis system would add $5.00 of overhead expense to the total line-item expenses ($80.00) resulting in $85.00 of expense for the account. The indirect cost for the product family reduces the profitability of the account.

Indirect costs are not necessarily applied to all product families / categories. Best practice is to allow the bank to establish the percentage for each category in the analysis system. A percentage of 0% would mean there simply is no additional indirect cost for the product category.

Yield On An Account Balance

When evaluating the profitability of a banking customer, some analysis systems will allow an account balance to be considered as part of the equation. While service costs and indirect expense for product categories will reduce the overall profitability of an account, the yield on an account balance (sometimes referred to as Funds Transfer Pricing), is an element of the equation that adds to an account's profitability.

Basically, a yield rate is used to calculate a balance yield which is added to an account's profitability. Using this concept, an account with a very large balance but low service activity may turn out to be more profitable than an account with a high volume of service activity but a low average balance. What an account balance means to the bank is represented by the yield rate. What's important in using this measurement of profitability is that all accounts are measured using the same rate. The profitability of an account then could be represented by:

Service Revenue (after service expense) + Yield on Account Balance – Indirect Costs

Summary - Calculating Profitability In Account Analysis

Service line-item cost factors may or may not be exact in account analysis. Some analysis solutions don't even support the concept of a cost factor for each service. Other analysis solutions support more than one cost factor for a single service. When used, cost factors are not exact in most cases. The same could be said for indirect cost factors and yields on collected balances. I maintain that it really doesn't matter because the intent in analysis is to measure and rank accounts, not see the exact profitability dollars made from each account. If the same cost factors are used in the measurement of all accounts, then the ranking of such accounts will be fairly accurate even though the costs may not be exact.

Account analysis solutions are principally designed to handle the billing of treasury management services, not the profitability of such, but having the capability of profitability ranking in the account analysis system is a bonus for the treasury management department. The ranking helps to identify which customers should be taken out to dinner vs. which customers need concession pricing removed. Concession pricing and fee waivers drive a customer's profitability down because all costs are present whether revenue is or not.

In the end, relying purely on account analysis for customer profitability reporting could be a slippery slope because the account analysis system normally has no insight into external activities of a customer, such as a customer's commercial lending activity.

Calculating Revenue Opportunity Lost

Some 15 years ago, I started speaking about something I called *Revenue Loss* in account analysis. I used this term to describe the amount of money being left on the table with banking customers due to discounts, concession pricing, and waivers, etc.

> *During a discussion at Columbia Bank in Tacoma, Washington, one of the meeting attendees pointed out to me that what I was describing was not Revenue Loss but Revenue Opportunity Loss. I immediately agreed with her synopsis and smiled inside because I knew on that day, in that meeting, a new financial acronym for account analysis was born (ROL). From that moment on, I used the term ROL in presentations and conversations. I still smile at facial expressions when I ask a banker "what was your ROL last month".*

I became very focused on this calculated value in account analysis because unlike other aspects of the billing system focused on revenue, ROL is focused on revenue that should be made but isn't. The term purely defines what could be a new revenue stream for a bank, if the bank would simply turn their attention toward the ROL value and take some action to recapture the ROL amount.

ROL is the calculated difference between the actual fees due for an account and the total fees that *would have been due* if only List Prices (and earnings rates) were used in the account analysis. Said another way, ROL is the calculated difference between an account's actual fees due and the fees that would have been due if there were no account exceptions whatsoever. Account exceptions that create ROL are account waiver Instructions, line-item service waiver instructions, any list price concessions for line-item services, and any other bottom-line discounts for product categories and/or bottom-line discounts on the account itself.

Today, some account analysis systems go to the trouble of calculating all accounts in analysis twice (once at actual price / earnings rate and once again using only list prices/rates). This re-calculation of all accounts shows the ROL then by service, account, and composite relationship. While this recalculation technique takes earnings allowance rate exceptions into consideration as well, the cost to do so means double the processing speed/time it takes to come up with such an analysis for each account in the first place.

Fine Tuning ROL

Arguably, one can make an argument for a similar value I personally call *Potential Revenue Loss* (e.g. PRL) which is just as meaningful as ROL. Potential Revenue Loss takes balances / earnings credit allowance out of the calculations. The PRL calculation at the service level simply compares the difference between List Price to Actual Price and doesn't require a complete recalculation of accounts and relationship summaries.

What I have found is that bank management is most concerned about revenue opportunity loss (due to discounts, etc.) over time. While discounts and waivers are often required in selling / onboarding new accounts, such exceptions should expire at some point and revert to standard pricing over time.

Both PRL and ROL are measuring sticks for monitoring by bank management. It is important to know that ROL is dramatically affected by the account balance and earnings credit each month. As a measuring tool, ROL is a bit of a slippery slope because the exact same service activity (and concessions) will result in different ROL amounts from month to month based upon balance level and earnings rate(s). PRL has tremendous merit because it is focused more on total exposure in service pricing (and the account balance means nothing). Both ROL and PRL are *memo calculations* but an effective means of measuring treasury management sales performance over time.

Summary – Calculating Revenue Opportunity Lost

The difference between PRL and ROL is so minor I have opted to not confuse the universe with two such terms, so I personally use ROL in all conversations (and this book) regarding the subject of lost opportunities. The fact is, while ROL is a *value of interest* some would say it is not *real*. By this I mean, a VP of Revenue Management would never go to senior management with a graph highlighting the ROL $ that the bank is losing. You see, account(s) making up the ROL $ possibly wouldn't even be at the bank without the special pricing afforded them in the first place.

In this light, ROL should be thought of more as a measuring tool or a key performance indicator, because the VP of Revenue Management would certainly want to know what treasury management salesperson has the most ROL attributed to them vs. all the other salespeople at the bank.

Because ROL is created by account exceptions, I think it is important to note that ROL will always be present in account analysis. As ROL is introduced into a bank's account analysis monthly process, it should also at some point leave the system too. Account level ROL will go away with the expiration of any associated account pricing exceptions.

Complex Calculations

While most service charge calculations in account analysis focus on a volume and a unit price, there are a collection of common service charges found in analysis that are not so easily calculated and therefore, sometimes difficult to understand.

Balance Assessment Fees

There are some well understood facts surrounding what is called the "FDIC Charge" found on Commercial Account Analysis statements. Most treasury professionals know the FDIC doesn't want an FI to use the word *FDIC* or *Insurance* in the service fee description on account analysis statements. Many FI's have opted for an alternative service description like *Balance Assessment Fee.* It should also be known that many FI's have removed this service fee from the analysis charges all together and are using alternative methods for compensation such as larger account maintenance fees & sometimes lower earnings allowance rates. I use the term *FDIC Charge* here because that is what it has long been known as in the industry.

For those FI's continuing to assess a service fee for "FDIC Charges", the most common practice is to base the fee on the average balance. Dividing this balance by 100 yields the # units (of $100) and this unit / volume is then the basis for a volume * price service fee calculation.

Unfortunately, some FDIC fee calculations have been made overly complicated by legacy systems attempting to mimic what the FDIC charges in assessing fees to the FI. Matching the FDIC calculation (which is based upon an FI's CAMELS rating) is virtually impossible and older account analysis systems attempting such, have only complicated matters.

Some of these systems treat the service price as an interest rate (and assess interest for the account balance). Other systems / FI's have set an annual unit price and then divide the charge by 12 months before assessing, often putting the words PER/YEAR in the service description. Few if ANY bank fees are stipulated as PER/YEAR so why the FDIC Assessment? Can you imagine a PAID CHECKS fee being assessed at 2.44 PER UNIT / PER YEAR?

If you are showing the likes of an FDIC Charge on your account analysis statement, the best practice is to base it on Units of $100 in Average Balance and set the unit price as you would any Volume * Price Service. The only remaining question then is how to treat the fee. While most FI's will show the fee as being compensable (offset by earnings allowance) one should think twice about that strategy.

What FI's aren't always thinking about is the corporate treasury professionals doing bank fee analysis. Their study often dives into the likes of FDIC Charges as well as other "balance based" services to determine their *real* earnings allowance rate on collected balances with an FI.

Imagine an account with a balance of $650k and an FDIC Charge of $65 for the month of October 2018. The FI may have committed to an ECR of 75 basis points (BPS) but if the FDIC Fee is compensable, that $65 fee will eat up approximately 12 BPS all by itself and the real ECR would be 63 BPS, not 75 BPS. Increasing the account balance wouldn't help because the FDIC Charge then increases and more of the earnings allowance is eaten alive.

I am personally an advocate for either eliminating the FDIC assessment all together (paid for by an increased account maintenance fee) or "hard charging" the FDIC assessment because a non-compensable service charge takes it completely out of the ECR evaluation being done in corporate treasury. An FI can easily soften the blow of hard charging the FDIC assessment by offering (and touting) higher ECR rates.

In the end, it is important for FI's to develop a strategy surrounding the likes of FDIC Charges and then implement that strategy. It is also important for FI's to update their brochures, disclosures, pro forma templates, RFP / RFI documents, etc. so that the FI strategy is clear, concise, and accurate. An FI's Account Analysis can be greatly simplified by eliminating the FDIC Charge all together and compensate for that loss using increased account maintenance fees instead. This approach will also fly under the radar screens of modern bank fee monitoring systems. It hardly makes sense to assess FDIC Charges on ONLY commercial account analysis customers anyway. Most importantly all FI's should take note, corporate treasury professionals are monitoring bank fees, and the FDIC Charge is only one of them!

The Earnings Credit Allowance

What is Your Real ECR?

Every treasury management banker should know that the ECR (Earnings Credit Rate) being touted by the bank for account analysis will at some point be scrutinized by what is called *bank fee monitoring*. There are consultancies in the business of helping businesses of all sizes with reducing their bank fees. While there are many spokes in the bicycle wheel of bank fee monitoring, at the hub is the ECR offered and advertised by the bank. If a bank is charging a *Balance Assessment Fee* (for many years called an FDIC charge) then one should know that in *bank fee monitoring*, the corporate treasurer (or their consultancy) will weigh any compensable *Balance Assessment Fees* against the bank ECR to determine the REAL earnings allowance being offered.

If this sounds a bit like account analysis post graduate work, it would be hard to argue otherwise. Some of the complexity is in how banks calculate the fee for the so-called *Balance Assessment Fee.* The fact is that most banks that charge a Balance Assessment Fee do so by applying a charge equal to $0.NN cents per/thousand dollars (or per/hundred dollars) of account balance. The bigger the balance, the bigger the service charge.

The issue at hand is that an ECR-Earnings Allowance Rate, is expressed as an annual percentage rate and the Balance Assessment Fee is typically a cents per/balance rate. Fourteen cents ($0.14) per one thousand dollars of balance is not the same as 14 Basis Points of ECR on the same Balance. Clearly, we need to get all the factors on the same playing field to perform an accurate comparison. The trick is to convert the cost of the Balance Assessment Fee into basis points because the service charge is balance based (just like the ECR). If we know that a *Balance Assessment Fee* is costing us 16 BPS each month and the bank is paying 55 BPS in earnings allowance each month, the truth is an account needs to look at their REAL earnings credit rate as possibly only 39 BPS.

For a *Balance Assessment Fee* charged at $0.14 per/one thousand dollars and an account balance of $1000, the charge will be $0.14 cents on the analysis statement. At 55 BPS the earnings allowance on that balance will be about $0.47 cents ($1000 * (.55% / 365) * 31). The $0.14 cents must be converted to BPS so we can determine how this fee will affect overall earnings. By taking the $0.14 cents and dividing it by the $1,000 balance, we can convert the service charge into BPS by applying the days in the analysis period and days in the year. The result here shows that $0.14 cents on $1000 in January 2021 is about 16 BPS (.00164838 = (((0.14/1000)/31) * 365)). While the treasury management services group at this bank may be touting an ECR of 55 BPS, the fact is, the real ECR is only about 39 BPS (16 BPS less) due to the bank's *Balance Assessment Fee.*

Now bankers should know that bank fee monitoring companies are telling businesses that there really should not be any Balance Assessment Fees (or Reserve Requirements) on their analysis statements anymore. Whether both are present or not, determining the real ECR a bank is paying may not be quite so easy as riding a bike.

Businesses going to banks with an RFP for treasury management services may be spinning their wheels around more than just a few times, to understand the real value of the ECR being offered at the hub.

Uncollected Funds Fees

Most account analysis systems employ the concept of bringing deposit accounts together and combining them into a single relationship view for commercial account billing. I am going to illustrate that the charges you see for Uncollected Funds Fees may not be as accurate as you think. Even modern corporate *bank fee monitoring tools* struggle calling this out, because the data commonly used for such analysis doesn't always see the whole picture.

For decades now, banks have touted the concept of commercial account relationship billing, where many depository accounts are brought together and viewed as one single customer. The benefits of this *customer-level* relationship view are many, in that all account balances are viewed as one and often achieve preferred earnings rates based upon tier levels.

Aggregated volumes from account activities (Deposits, Wires, ACH Items, etc.) often receive tiered volume discounts on service charges simply because of the aggregated volume levels in a relationship of several accounts. With domestic treasury services and commercial account analysis, balances play a major role because the earnings allowance is based upon balances.

One of the more interesting balance-based fees in commercial billing is known as the *Uncollected Funds Fee*. Commercial banks typically charge a loan rate (e.g. Prime plus 3% to 4%) on average collected balance overdrafts for a given month. A collected balance overdraft on any given day of the month, for any account in a relationship can trigger this bank fee. A savvy treasury management salesperson would likely tell their corporate client / prospect not to worry about the *Uncollected Funds Fee* because the positive balances in one account of the relationship will have the opportunity to offset the uncollected funds that arise in another account.

Only a savvy corporate treasurer will ask, "how are the account balances all brought together?" because that has a dramatic effect on daily Uncollected Funds. The short answer to this question lies within the capabilities of the commercial billing system being used by each bank. There are two basic methods of combining many account balances together for a single customer view.

One method is to take the end of month average balances for each account in a relationship and simply add them together, this is referred to as a *Monthly Balance Aggregation*. Most analysis systems use this approach for commercial billing when there is limited system functionality to do otherwise.

The second method is to take the *daily* ending balances of all accounts in a relationship and add them all together each day, then form an average balance of the entire relationship *at* the end of the month using the DAILY results, this is often referred to as a *Daily Balance Offset*.

Both methods will derive the exact same Average NET Balance at the end of the month. When it comes to Average Positive Balance though (upon which earnings allowance is normally based) and Average Negative Balance (upon which the Uncollected Funds Fee is normally based), these two methods of bringing deposit account balances together couldn't be more divergent.

The illustration below shows a sample relationship of 2 deposit accounts over a period of just 4 days. When you do the math, you will notice that the *Average NET Balance* of $1,250 for the whole relationship is the same regardless of Monthly / Daily Balance offset methods. It is the Average Negative Balance that derives the Uncollected Funds Fee though.

		DDA Accounts for ABC Industries		ABC Industries Relationship Summary	
				End of Month	Daily
	Day #	111	222	Offset	Offset
	1	$ 10,000	$ 5,000	n/a	$ 15,000
	2	$ (7,500)	$ 5,000	n/a	$ (2,500)
	3	$ (7,500)	$ 10,000	n/a	$ 2,500
	4	$ (7,500)	$ (2,500)	n/a	$ (10,000)
Aggregate Net		$ (12,500)	$ 17,500	$ 5,000	$ 5,000
Aggregate Positive		$ 10,000	$ 20,000	$ 30,000	$ 17,500
Aggregate Negative		$ (22,500)	$ (2,500)	$ (25,000)	$ (12,500)
Average Net		$ (3,125)	$ 4,375	$ 1,250	$ 1,250
Average Positive		$ 2,500	$ 5,000	$ 7,500	$ 4,375
Average Negative		$ (5,625)	$ (625)	$ (6,250)	$ (3,125)
Earnings Credit @ 50 BPS				$ 0.41	$ 0.24
Uncollected Funds Charge @ 8.25%				$ 5.65	$ 2.83

Using the Daily Balance Offset approach to combining accounts clearly shows the Average Negative Balance for this sample relationship is much smaller than what is shown for a Monthly Balance Aggregation approach.

One can argue the Monthly Balance Aggregation approach is overcharging ABC Industries for Uncollected Funds. The Average Positive Balance is lower with a Daily Balance Offset (it is because it was used to cover overdrawn days), but the lower Average Positive balance is getting an earnings credit rate that is 16 times smaller than the Uncollected Funds Fee rate.

The truth of the matter is that very few commercial billing systems in the world today have the functional capability of calculating a Daily Balance Offset, so banks are put into a position where they have little choice but to revert to the Monthly Balance Aggregation approach or not charge for Uncollected Funds at all. In today's world of instant access to online banking and real time payments, ABC Industries is paying an Uncollected Funds Fee that is higher than what they should be paying simply because the billing system does NOT see the whole customer relationship DAILY.

This fee-inflation can also fly under the radar of *bank fee monitoring* tools because these corporate treasury tools often don't have a clear line of sight to the daily ending balance positions of each deposit account. Some banks simply use the NET Collected Balance to charge an Uncollected Funds Fee (and then calculate an earnings allowance with it too). Both these alternatives are considered bad practices because an OD charge develops only if the average for the entire month is overdrawn. On the earnings side, an account is being penalized at the ECR rate for overdrawn balances melded into the NET.

Other banks have opted to simply not charge for uncollected funds to avoid the technology / calculation shortcomings. Without a daily balance offset capability, these banks are paying too much in earnings allowance as well (e.g. the Average Positive Balances are being **overstated** in situations where there are draws into uncollected funds).

The bottom line is that an Uncollected Funds Fee can be enormous, the calculation for it needs to be 100% accurate. Even small errors in the calculation of an earnings allowance can add up to large dollars when it comes to fee income for a bank. Commercial billing involves many details, so it needs to be clear, concise, and accurate.

Using a Daily Balance Offset for relationship summary billing is absolutely the most accurate and transparent approach. Unfortunately for large corporate entities, bank billing systems and "*bank fee monitoring*" systems, may not have all the facts readily available to calculate, verify, and audit such fees.

Hybrid Account Analysis

In an era of higher interest rates mixed with a bank's propensity to retain / grow deposit balances, it is no wonder why more banks are now offering business checking accounts interest on account balances. The concept is simple, but the subject becomes a bit more complex when these same accounts use treasury management services too, meaning these business accounts are a part of the bank's account analysis and commercial billing operation. While Interest Credit Rates (ICRs) are at the heart of paying interest on deposits, Earnings Credit Rates (ECRs) are used to offset bank fees in account analysis. Interestingly, both rates are focused on the same checking account balance.

The most common approach to paying hard interest (based on an ICR), is to use the demand deposit daily (or average daily) balance and calculate a monthly interest payment. Because credit has already been provided to the checking account in this scenario, the bank would not want to provide additional credit for the same balance in the form of an account analysis earnings allowance (based on ECR). It would seem easy enough to change the ECR in the analysis system to a zero rate, so no additional credit is allowed on the same balance. The account analysis system being used though must support such a move.

Account analysis can introduce complexity to the situation if the deposit account in question is a part of a family relationship of accounts, where a bank typically groups several deposit accounts together to apply an ECR at the relationship summary level (often with tiered ECRs). It may not be possible to zero an ECR on a single member of a family relationship, which could leave the bank (perhaps unknowingly) providing additional credit on the same interest- bearing deposit account. Luckily, some account analysis systems support the concept of designating a deposit account as interest-bearing, so the balance is not included in the relationship summary earnings allowance calculations.

I was once told, "make sure you have a system that does all that you need it to do and then control that system. If you don't do this, an alternative system will evolve on its own, and it will control you".

I think of this advice when I think of banks using account analysis systems that don't have the features needed to properly deal with ICR's and ECR's. I've seen first-hand banks trying to offset the effect of an earnings allowance being calculated on an account balance that has already been paid interest in the deposit system. Some banks will send the interest paid in DDA as a service charge into account analysis, others will send the interest paid in DDA as an adjustment to any earnings allowance calculated in account analysis. In either of these scenarios, I like to suggest banks be sure to include a phone number right within the description of any such line-item entries.

I am an advocate for account analysis system features that allow a product management team to do whatever it is they want to do. Gaining in popularity is the concept of *hybrid* analysis, a concept that has been used on non-profit accounts for many years, long before Dodd-Frank ever made paying interest on business checking, legal. The idea behind hybrid analysis is to not pay interest from the DDA system at all but instead, use the account analysis system to pay any/all interest on the account.

The word *"hybrid"* is often used because the earnings allowance (based on ECR) in such a scenario is used to cover all the compensable bank fees and then any excess available balance (along with an ICR) is used to compute an interest credit back to the deposit account. This approach removes any need to adjust an earnings allowance by interest paid from another system. There is no need to force zero rates or mark an account separately as interest bearing. It also allows for the negotiation of both ICR and ECR for any given situation. A higher ECR is going to result in a lower balance required to offset fees, and thus more interest credit.

Balances change every month, and so will the analysis results. A tiered structure ICR or ECR can also become a factor in the negotiation. A bank can also reduce the need for line-item service discounts and waivers, if the entire negotiation process turns to a tiered ECR and/or ICR.

I have found that some banks make good use of the account analysis tools they have, features that put them in control of something like interest-bearing products. I have also found other banks who are answering customer phone calls trying to explain how the interest credit on a checking account statement is being used as an adjustment on the account analysis statement, because they couldn't avoid the bank's ECR providing an allowance on the same deposit balances. Account analysis is complicated enough, so it is important to take control of the system. My advice is "don't let an analysis system lacking in processing features evolve into multiple tasks where the *"work arounds"*, now control you".

Revenue Enhancement - Without Raising Prices

It seems the concept of revenue enhancement captures the attention of most people surrounding account analysis and billing. There is a great deal of subject matter surrounding account analysis that can assist with revenue enhancement. When it comes to increasing revenue, most people think of raising prices, but I like to focus on revenue enhancement ideation where standard pricing is left untouched. Following then, are key subject matter ideas for increasing bank revenue, without raising standard prices.

Fee Based Services

You might call them hard charges or explicit charges. Some call them Fee Based charges. The AFP-Association for Financial Professionals sometimes refers to them as Non-Compensable Fees. Whatever you call them, they will absolutely increase a bank's Treasury Management bottom line revenue.

Where to Focus

By default, most analysis systems are going to treat line-item service charges as being compensable, meaning they can be offset by the account balance and calculated earnings allowance achieved, using that balance. These services are easily recognized on analysis statements because with most AA systems, they have a *Balance Requirement* shown to the right of the service charge amount.

When trying to choose which services should be fee-based (non-compensable), it is important to look at the bank's cost because the higher the cost of a service, the easier it is to explain the reasoning behind making a service non-compensable.

While many bankers will tell you they don't really know their exact cost of a TM service, there are certain services where the costs are very high, even as high as 100% of the charge, you might know them as *3rd Party Services* or *Pass Through* services. In essence, these services are charged to the bank by a 3rd Party (e.g. Brinks Armored Car Services), paid for by the bank in real dollars, and passed on to the bank's customers who are responsible for the charges being generated in the first place. All too often however, these services are allowed as compensable in account analysis and therefore may or may not actually be collected from the customer(s).

Another focus area is uncollected funds. Most FI's have an uncollected funds fee which is a charge for drawing into uncollected funds (aka. a negative collected balance at the end of the day). Because an earnings allowance is provided for positive daily balances no matter what, the uncollected funds fee for a negative end of day collected balance should be charged no matter what. In my opinion, uncollected funds fees should justifiably be non-compensable.

Service Status / Fee Disposition

It should be noted that not all account analysis systems support hard charges for specific line-item services in account analysis. If your bank is using one of these systems for commercial billing, you are long overdue for a software update.

The data element you need to look at in account analysis is often called *Service Status* or *Service Fee Disposition*. At the service level, you simply change the service status / disposition from A-Analyzed to whatever code your system uses to indicate F-*Fee Based* / or non-compensable.

Results to DDA

When passing these service charges to the DDA system, some systems lump analyzed services together with non-analyzed services and form a single service charge transaction. Other systems allow these charges to be sent separately as two DDA debit transactions. Clearly, one approach is more transparent than the other.

Non-Monthly Compensation Cycles

If a bank supports quarterly or annual compensation cycles for account analysis, you might find that the analysis system will automatically debit these accounts for fee-based services monthly, even though the compensation cycle is quarterly, for example.

The rationale for this is that non-compensable service fees are due no matter what, so there is no reason to wait until the end of a quarter to charge an account for a fee-based service that is generated every month. The ECR means nothing for fee-based services (a $25 fee that occurs in January is still going to be $25 assessed at the end of the quarter because it cannot be offset).

> *A Treasury salesperson once told me about a bank that touted "bank with us, we offer the best ECR's in the valley". When I asked how they can afford to do that he replied, "very easily, they hard charge the Balance Assessment Fee". Another officer told me about a bank that touted "bank with us, we have no Balance Assessment Fees here". When I asked how they can afford to do that he replied, "easily, they had the worst ECR's in the valley"!*

Waived Accounts

If a bank supports the concept of Waived Accounts, you might find that fee-based services are not always waived. Some analysis systems have an option setting that controls the behavior of fee-based services for Waived Accounts. These options control whether such fees are in fact charged or waived.

Summary - Fee Based Services

There are certainly other areas to focus on when it comes to non-compensable services. In any case, you might find the bottom-line revenue increase from using this revenue enhancement technique, to be staggering.

Recapture Waived Fees

Whether a bank is waiving a single line-item service or an entire account relationship, the waived fees are perhaps the costliest of bank concessions, and I am a strong advocate for taking care of the big rocks first.

What if a bank could recapture even a portion of all the fees currently being waived? The result would surely be an enhancement to bottom line revenue. Fee waivers should attract the attention of finance because when it comes to revenue enhancement, fee waivers may likely be the biggest boulders in the bank.

Call Them What They Are

The concept of recapturing waived fees might become clearer once we stop calling them *Waivers*. More simply said, *Waivers* are 100% discounts. When a line-item service is waived, we are basically mapping a 100% discount to the service. To make matters worse for the bank, many account analysis systems force users to set up an exception price (a unit price of $0.00) to achieve the 100 % discount. Such an exception makes matters worse because an exception price of $0.00 calculates a charge of $0.00 and the bank has no idea how much in service fees are being given away by the waiver. Most analysis systems do not show $0.00 charge items on analysis statements.

The best practice (if your analysis system allows) for handling such exceptions is to leave standard pricing as is and identify a service waive some other way (e.g. a service status or fee disposition), so that a charge will be computed. Using this technique, everyone (including the customer) sees the actual value of the 100% discount.

I've never been a treasury management salesperson in my life, but I love to pose the question, "what treasury services salesperson couldn't sell a customer on an 80% discount, or even a 60% discount"?

To be sure, a service with a waived fee disposition on an analysis statement will at least let the customer know they are currently getting something for free. The best practice would be to first show customers that value before applying any discount of less than 100%.

Account Level Waivers

Waiving all fees for an account or customer traditionally has been a little more transparent than line-item services. The total fees due after earnings credit are simply cast aside and not charged to the customer (but at least one can see what they are).

I think the most common problem with account level waiver instructions is that they remain forever. The best practice would be to have an annual review process where the analysis account is evaluated periodically, and changes are made as necessary.

A bank's analysis system will likely need to support bottom line discounting if the bank is going to claw back on waived account fees (as I am suggesting). While some systems allow an account to be entirely waived, they don't always allow one to remove the waive instruction and instead, apply an 80% discount to the bottom-line fees due.

Recapture the ROL

Whether dealing with service line-item waivers or account waivers, the best practice would be to have a recapture process in place. All the 100% discounts should likely be adjusted to something less with annual account reviews, and through time, eventually go away. Removing waivers entirely can certainly be done when doing an account review but likely not without creating customer angst (as seen by cable television & cell phone providers).

> *A large midwestern bank holding company once showed me they had $200k in monthly fee waivers across their account base. Clawing back on those waivers to instead offer 80% discounts meant increasing monthly revenue by almost $40k per/month in the first year. Having this first-hand experience convinced me that an account analysis system capable of bottom-line discounts along with other automated claw back features, would simply pay for itself.*

How Big is the Problem?

Sometimes the best path forward in fixing a problem is to first understand just how large the problem is in the first place. Waived fees are just one component of what I refer to as ROL-Revenue Opportunity Lost. Understanding your ROL from waived accounts and waived fees is important. My suggestion is to begin implementing this revenue enhancement by identifying the total value of monthly waived accounts and services. If the bank is waiving fees with $0.00 value exception pricing instructions, coming up with an accurate view of ROL will be a bit more challenging and require a deeper dive.

Summary – Recapture Waived Fees

Increasing bottom-line revenue using this revenue enhancement technique can often have significant impact for a financial institution. I sometimes like to say, "it all begins, with someone who cares".

Zero Priced Account Exceptions

Waivers are often obfuscated by account exceptions with the unit price set to $0.00 (zero). Savvy treasury management sales officers have learned that when an exception is created with a zero price, the service will fly for free under the radar. With a focus on identity and then eventual recapture, a bank will absolutely increase their Treasury Management bottom line revenue.

Understand the Difference

While the result is essentially the same, there is a colossal difference between a service Waiver in account analysis and a service exception / instruction with the unit price set to $0.00 (zero). While both are 100% discounts, the difference between the two is one of transparency.

A service Waiver in analysis is clearly shown on the analysis statement. The AFP standards for statement formatting recommend that banks show a "W" next to any line-item service charge that is being waived. The key here is that a charge has been calculated and is being reported, but it is not actually being charged. Everyone though, can see how much the service charge is.

A service exception placed on an account with a unit price set to $0.00 (zero) calculates a service charge of $0.00 (zero). The issue is most analysis systems will not show a $0.00 (zero) service charge on the customer statement. With a calculated result of $0.00 (zero), the bank has no idea what this service exception / instruction is costing them. At least with service Waivers, one can tell what they all add up to.

> *A premium account analysis solution will likely allow a user to stipulate that a specific service with an actual volume should be shown on the analysis statement, even if the calculated service charge turns out to be zero. This selective display capability is not often seen throughout the industry.*

Changing Zero Priced Exceptions to Service Waivers

The best practice (if your analysis system allows) for handling $0.00 (zero) priced exceptions is to use a service Waiver instruction instead. This is typically done with what is called a fee disposition or a service status. Given a unit price, a service charge will be computed. Using this technique, everyone (including the customer) sees the actual value of the 100% discount.

Once it becomes very clear a customer is getting a 100% discount on a service, a treasury team can go to work on recapturing what I call ROL-Revenue Opportunity Lost. More on this subject can be found in my February newsletter.

Left with only a computed service charge of $0.00 (zero) however, no one in the bank knows how big this problem is. These zero priced exceptions are typically not seen by anyone except those in the back office of the bank. A service with a waived fee disposition on a statement will at least let the customer know they are currently getting something for free.

Recapture the Associated ROL

Whether dealing with service line-item waivers or zero priced service exceptions, the best practice would be to have a recapture process in place. Any 100% discount should likely be adjusted to something less than 100%.

Services with a $0.00 (zero) unit price are just one component of what I refer to as ROL-Revenue Opportunity Lost. They may or may not even be present in your system today. You might find there are an overwhelming number of them. If you find too many to deal with, then focus on specific service codes one at a time.

A great best practice would be to never allow such instructions to be entered into your system in the first place because if they are entered into the system, they are often hidden there forever.

Summary – Zero Priced Account Exceptions

When ending account analysis presentations, I sometimes tell people here is something you can do right now to improve your monthly revenue, and you don't necessarily need a new analysis system to do it.

Firstly, don't ever let a price exception of $0.00 into your system because they fly too low under the radar. Secondly, identify any service price exceptions in the current system where the unit price is $0.00 (zero). Change the price exceptions to service Waivers or alternatively, go right to work on ROL recapture by setting the unit price to some percentage of the service's LIST price. Tell those that are impacted, we simply cannot offer 100% discounts forever.

Tiered ECRs

A Tiered Rate Approach

If you've worked with account analysis systems in banks for as long as I have, you remember the days of 5% earnings allowance rates. Back then it was difficult to determine who your best treasury management customers were because most accounts were not deriving any (non-interest) fee income, the account service fees were all swallowed up by the soft credit allowed on the customer's net invest-able funds.

As interest rates began plummeting (the slow downward slide started in 2000), the earnings allowance rates used in account analysis eventually became a small concern. With little in the way of soft credits, most analysis customers fell into a deficit position and the thought of even tweaking the earnings allowance rate simply didn't make sense. For the last several years now, the commercial billing process inside financial institutions has evolved into more of an operational (or clinical) exercise vs. an account analysis process. Let's face it, there isn't much *analysis* to be performed with the likes of 0% earnings rates. Most banks have been simply running their billing systems and closing their monthly process in a rush to auto debit the accounts (interesting to note that only in treasury management departments do banks *"sign their customers up"* for monthly auto payments whether they like it or not).

With interest rates starting to inch up (a trend that started in 2015), financial institutions need to rethink their monthly commercial billing process to maximize (non-interest) income from treasury management services. Suffice to say, *"set it and forget it"* is not a good strategy when it comes to the earnings allowance rate in account analysis.

The first thing every financial institution should do (if not doing already), is move to a tiered rate approach for the earnings credit rate. If a bank is offering a single non-tiered earnings credit rate to their customers, I often say that the bank is offering their very best rate to everyone. The idea here is to *NOT* offer your best earnings allowance rate to everyone. Instead, only the best customers should get the best rate. The commercial account average collected balance should determine the earnings rate a customer receives (based upon a tiered structure). The balance levels and basis point differences in the rate tier will certainly take a little *internal* ***analysis*** but the result will pay for itself.

Assume for a moment that Commercial National Bank of Your Town has 2,000 accounts to be billed each month in *account analysis* and the average balance across all these accounts is $150k. Assuming the top 20% of the accounts will get the best earnings rate offered by the bank, the remaining 1,600 would receive something *less.* Doing some simple math, even 5 basis points on $50k would be $2.12 (.0005/365) * $50k * 31 Days). Using these presumptions, CNB would have a very good chance of increasing fee income by over $3k monthly (1,600 * $2.12) simply by tweaking the lower earnings credit rate tier by 5 basis points.

Now what if the rate difference was 10 BPS? What if there were multiple balance splits in the tiered structure creating larger rate differentials? As rates rise, so does the potential gap for larger rate differences in each of the balance tiers. This tiered approach could even allow for *higher* rates than normal at the very highest balance levels (paid for by accounts in the lower tiers).

Summary – Tiered ECR's

Any financial institution would want to look closely at potential balance tiers and the resulting effects on bottom-line fee income. Balance levels should remain static (so customers don't have a moving target). Earnings rates however were designed to *fluctuate,* normally with the 91 Day T-Bill rate. Altering the earnings allowance rate monthly for an FI's billing process should soon again become the norm. Then again, isn't that why we call it account analysis?

Missing Service Fees

Most Treasury Management products offered by financial institutions are paid for by assessing recurring maintenance fees to customers who use such products. An internal audit of all such fees will often reveal something customers will not call their bank about, that being the monthly recurring maintenance fee is missing.

When I think of bank fee monitoring systems and the steps taken to discover billing issues, one that quickly comes to mind is the search for accounts that only have monthly maintenance fees (no activity-based fees). These situations develop when a deposit account is no longer being used by a business. Until closed or discovered, recurring maintenance fees typically continue to be assessed on such accounts for months on end. This is why monitoring systems are looking for this situation in the first place.

When one thinks of missing monthly maintenance fees, the search to be performed is the exact opposite of our bank fee monitoring example. The search is for all accounts that have activity for a particular treasury product, but they are missing the recurring fee.

As an example, one can assume an account is actively using the bank's ACH Origination product, if the account in question is showing ACH Originated Debits / Credits for the month. If an account is indeed active for the month, there most certainly should be a recurring monthly maintenance fee for the ACH Origination service. A banker once said to me, "Well, we waive the maintenance fee for some customers". This is perfectly understandable, but my response would be that the *ACH Origination Maintenance Fee* should still be present, it would just happen to be waived. Without a maintenance fee service present at all, it leaves one to think about whether it was waived or simply forgotten.

Finding the Missing Fees

In the perfect world, an account analysis system would have built in functionality to easily identify customer situations where service fees are missing. Lacking this ability, one could still accomplish a rather effective search as follows:

- **First:** Create a spreadsheet of all accounts with an *ACH Origination Maintenance Fee* service. You can likely focus on the specific service code for this fee. Sort your worksheet by account number and call this worksheet Table A.

- **Second:** Create a second spreadsheet of all accounts using any of the service codes that would be considered account activity (ACH Credits, ACH Debits, ACH Files, etc.). Call this worksheet Table B.

- For Table B, you really want just a distinct list of account numbers with ACH service activity so using Excel filtering, you can create a list of distinct account numbers.

- **Third:** Using Table B, you can now do an Excel V-Lookup on the maintenance fee account list in Table A. If you have any *not found* account numbers, you will have discovered accounts having ACH activity (Table B) but are missing the ACH Origination Maintenance service.

- **Finally:** It is suggested you rinse and repeat this process for all Treasury Management Products including Lockbox, Positive Pay, RDC, Online Banking, and more.

Accounting for Exception Situations

As some analysis systems use relationship summary numbers to link accounts together in a relationship, you may want to include the relationship summary number (if applicable) in your Table A and Table B extracts. This way, if the ACH Origination service is only charged once per/relationship, you will be able to see whether a customer is indeed being charged correctly for the service. As mentioned earlier, if the service fee is missing due to it being waived, the best practice would be to put the waiver on the statement for all to see.

Missing Service Fees – Summary

Ideally, the internal onboarding process for accounts and products would never allow the situation described above to ever develop. Still, through conversions, system consolidations, mergers, acquisitions, etc. recurring fees often do slip through the cracks. Banking customers are never going to call and complain about a missing fee though. Running through an internal audit like this (with all TM products) can be a very healthy exercise for revenue enhancement. As is true for so many revenue enhancement ideas, "someone has to care".

Align & Sundown Pricing Concessions

There is absolutely nothing wrong with pricing concessions in account analysis. Concession pricing has long been a part of selling Treasury Management Services and everyone is happy when a new deal is signed. While concession pricing is a necessary strategy to win new business and onboard new customers, without proper controls in place the unfortunate end results of such concessions are a major blow to potential revenue.

When one thinks of standard list pricing as compared to concession pricing, the real difference between them is something I call ROL-*Revenue Opportunity Lost.* I literally gave a presentation some years ago where I candidly stated that I made up a new financial acronym: ROL. Imagine the look on one's face when I ask them, "so what is your monthly ROL?".

It seems the biggest problem with concession pricing is that it seldom goes away. Once planted into the basement of the billing system, it often remains there forever. Even when reviewed over time, the decisioning tends to lean towards leaving the concession as is or removing it entirely, with no consideration of simply *clawing back (aka.* making the effort to get closer to the list price).

I have no doubt that when concession pricing is approved and used for one new customer, it becomes a bit of a sales strategy for future potential customers, thereby multiplying exponentially throughout a financial institution. Like compound interest, ROL becomes even larger as standard list prices change over time because the concessions most often remain static.

Consider a concession price for a common service: ***Paid Checks.*** According to a 2018 study, small businesses issue an average of 34 checks per/month. If the standard list price is $0.22 per/item and a new customer just onboarded is granted a concession price of $0.15 per/item, the ROL on one check is $0.07. Using this SMB average, the FI's ROL for one service, one account, and one month is $2.38. What if the business was not so small? What if more than one service had such a concession?

It's likely a unit price like this could quickly spread to 500 accounts or more which could mean ROL of $1,190 a month and over $14k per/year. This illustration wouldn't be so bad if the concessions on these accounts all expired after 12 months. As happens all too often though the concessions never expire, they multiply instead.

In the end, the service volume, concession value, account volume, and most importantly time, all contribute to ROL-Revenue Opportunity Lost.

ROL = 1 service X # units X $ concession X # accounts X # months

If you're a Treasury Management Product Manager or responsible in any way for Treasury Revenue Management, please note from the above that time is not on your side. In fact, *time* plays a major role in contributing to ROL.

The answer to eliminating long term ROL is expiration dates for concession pricing. Concession pricing at some point, should come to an end. While special pricing is completely understood for winning new business, continuing it on forever is simply bad business. Waivers are certainly the costliest of concession pricing, they are 100% discounts. I have never been a treasury salesperson in my life, but I ask, "what treasury management salesperson couldn't sell a service at an 80% discount"?

Best practice is to assign an expiration date (aka. review date) to any pricing concession. Treasury management officers should get alerts in advance of those dates so that there is time for decisioning. The decision should be to remove the concession entirely, or claw back on it partially.

In some cases, the pricing concessions end up having a variety of expiration dates, even for a single account. Premium account analysis solutions support the concept of alignment. While an account is being reviewed and a detailed analysis is done for several pricing concessions, any continuation of such concessions is typically aligned to a new expiration / renewal date where they can all be reviewed at once.

All too often in the treasury management industry, the concession prices become very much like the most famous infomercial tag line ever used, "Just Set It and Forget It".

Concession Pricing Approval Workflows

While concession pricing absolutely is here to say with account analysis, it doesn't mean there shouldn't be guardrails and/or a workflow approval process in place to control the creation of special pricing.

The best practice is to propose special pricing using a proforma model showing the anticipated balances, volumes, and fees. Any deviation from list price would be reflected in such a model. Key performance indicators within the proforma like margin, realization, ROL, etc. would be the basis for anyone making an approval decision for exception pricing. The first question is always, "how much of a discount are actually proposing"?

Once a proposal is prepared, it should go through the planned approval process for the discount values being proposed. The best practice is to have a value-based approval process because the value of the overall discount should define the type of approval process that should be required. Waiving the fees for an entire account is quite different than a 20% discount off the *Wire Transfer* product category of services.

Surcharge Pass Through Fees

When billing files are posted to the analysis accounts, the process typically involves the posting of volumes or actual charges. When the transaction stipulates a charge / dollar amount vs. a volume, the service is referred to as a flat fee (or a pre-priced service). A billing file containing a check-printing fee (expressed as dollars and cents) for example, would have transactions on it that depict a unique charge amount for each account. Another example might be a file containing charges for armored car services. These transactions typically contain a unique charge amount that was calculated by another system. These fees are then paid by the bank to the 3rd party vendor (the armored car services company in this example).

It is best and common practice for these fees to be passed on to the accounts responsible for the charges in the first place. By passing these third-party fees on to the accounts who instantiated them, the bank is automatically re-imbursed for their payment to the third-party vendor (well, sort of). If the fees being passed through to analysis are set up as compensable services, an account's balance might compensate for some of the charge. It is important to understand in this situation that the bank is paying the vendor but may NOT get entirely re-imbursed if such services are compensable. Certainly, a bank could set up such fees as non-compensable, but that is a different revenue enhancement technique described earlier in this section.

The best practice is to have the account analysis system surcharge these flat charges to cover any expense involved with administering them in the first place. If a Check Printing Charge of $18.00 came into the system for posting to an account, the account analysis system should allow a surcharge of 10% to be applied automatically.

The actual charge to the customer would then be $19.80 [$18.00 + (10% of $18.00)]. Surcharging such fees will create a higher level of profitability for the bank.

If these pass-through fees are not set up as fee-based / hard charged in the analysis system, the surcharge can help cover the cost incurred by the bank paying such fees in real dollars while passing the charge on to the banking customers as being balance compensable. This would be considered common practice.

Revenue Enhancement - Summary

In Treasury Management Services Billing, the term *WAIVED* is quite often used. As of late, I try to use terminology describing exactly what this really means. A Waiver is a 100% discount. The 100% discounts become very costly when you consider the fact these waivers are often placed on accounts and remain there forever (without an expiration date). Very costly too are line-item services being waived. These service waivers are often placed without any meaningful expiration date.

Waived service fees at the line-item level in account analysis are stealth in nature because they have no financial impact on account analysis itself. Waived line-item services are not a part of any meaningful analysis calculations because they are basically shown on a statement and thrown out of any results. If you look closely at an analysis statement and have your calculator handy, you'll find the waived line-item service fees are simply shown and forgotten about.

Services with a unit price of zero are even worse because in these cases, while we are still dealing with a 100% discount, we have no idea of what the overall amount is being given away. If we were to sit back and look at the total of all such waivers, service after service, account after account, month after month, most would find the totals disturbing. Most finance departments in financial institutions are focused on fee income making it in the front door (and perhaps being lost out the back door due to expenses) vs. the waived fees (the 100% service discounts) which are literally blowing out the side windows. These are all revenue opportunities lost each month.

At the risk of stating the obvious, the solution to any problem is first realizing there is a problem and then understanding how big that problem is. Perhaps the best solution to such problems is determining how we got to where we are in the first place and then making procedural changes to mitigate that issue.

One suggestion is to dive into the lowest level of detail, the services. Are there price exceptions with a unit price of zero? One could only estimate how much these are costing the bank. Are there line-item service waivers? Do they ever expire? What are they adding up to each month? The total of line-item service waivers for a given month would need to be added to any/all account level waivers. How much in account level fees are being waived each month? Do they ever expire? All of these are 100% discounts. Are we capable of selling clients on something less, an 80% discount perhaps? What business would pack their bags and leave the bank because all you would give them is an 80% discount?

As treasury management salespeople are out selling products to new / existing customers (bringing that fee income into the front door), the prudent Director of Treasury Management Services should be taking a walk around the institution looking for expiration dates and closing the side windows.

Eight

Monthly Operations

Data Collection and Posting

Account analysis data is collected from numerous file sources. The primary input to any analysis system is the core demand deposit system. Best practice is to have the core deposit system feed the analysis system with account information daily. The daily data includes service volumes, account ending balances, and any changes to name/address or other account demographics (branch, region, market, cost center, account type code, etc.). Most importantly, new accounts opened in the core deposit system must get to the account analysis system as quickly as possible.

While billing data can be sent to account analysis each day, most often files containing service billing data are sent to account analysis at the end of a month. This billing data is commonly referred to as ancillary billing information or 3rd Party Billing Files. The reason for this terminology is that banks often use their core vendor for certain treasury management products, but they also use different vendors for other treasury management products. In either case, the billing data is funneled into the account analysis system.

The illustration that follows shows sample treasury management products that send account activity (volumes and charges) to account analysis for commercial billing.

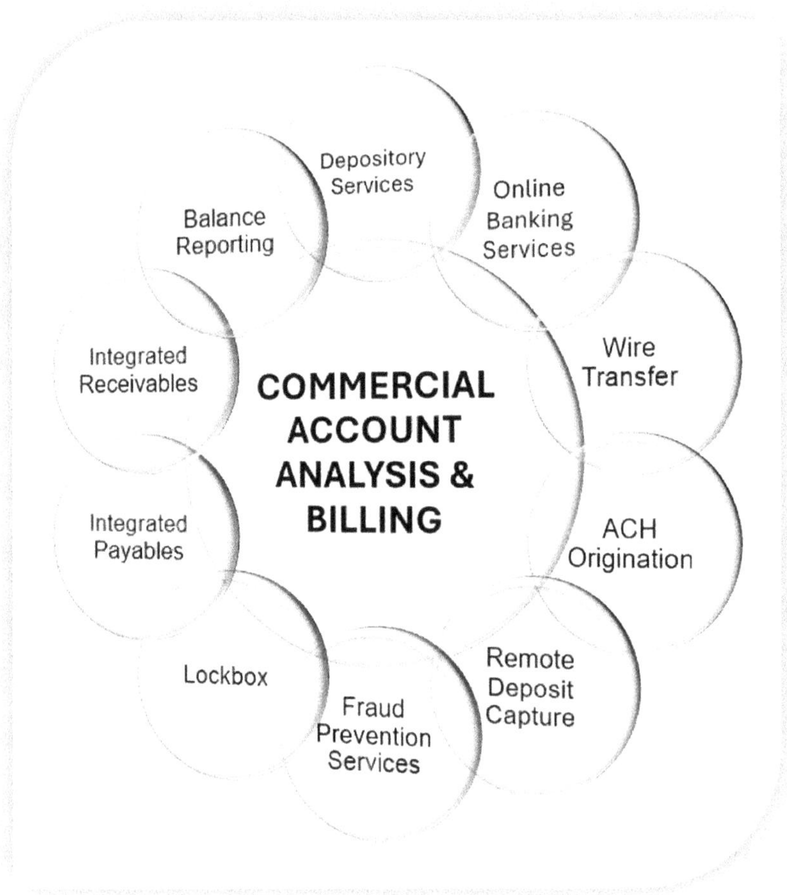

To help operational users, the best practice for any/all files being processed would be to describe / document the files in a file catalogue or file library (e.g. a *File Description*) so users understand what each file contains, where it comes from (the file source) and the nature of the billing data on the file.

From an operations perspective, the analysis system should LEARN what is normal for each file in terms of records or hash totals (this way the data collection process could highlight any abnormality). Recognizing and understanding the data files being processed each month for analysis is subject matter for *Machine Learning.*

When service billing files are processed by the data collection and posting process, the best practice for the transactions on such billing files would be to have these transactions identified by a File ID, identifying the original file they came into the system on. The reason for this is that there will come a time when a file needs to be un-posted or removed from the data collection.

> *In some analysis systems today, a user is forced to post a volume reversal file to un-post data whereas they should be able to easily ELIMINATE a file of transactions altogether at the click of a button. Just imagine the user steps involved in creating a volume reversal file.*

The best practice for 3rd party billing files is to include an effective date and a service code, along with the File ID. The service code identifies what a volume being reported represents. Service code **ABCD1234** for example, might be used by a 3rd party sender of data to represent the volume for *Paid Checks*. An effective date becomes important because it will dictate which billing period a particular transaction count pertains to. It is common for someone to be posting data and working on the billing for the month of June 2025, well into July 2025. The most common elements to consider for a 3rd party billing file then are:

-**File Type ID:** Identifies the type of file being posted as defined in the file catalog/library

-File ID: Identifies which file an item originated from

-Bank Number: Identifies the bank where the account exists

-Account Number: Identifies the account to post the transaction to

-Effective Date: MM/DD/YYYY of the transaction

-Service Code: Identifies the service line item / billing point

-Volume Count or Charge: Normally a whole number but could be a flat fee (or fractional number)

One of the struggles in account analysis operations has to do with research. Someone will see a bank fee on a statement that doesn't make any sense to them. They then need to research where the volume / bank fee came from. Imagine knowing the File Type, File ID, Service Code, and Account Number for every line-item on an analysis statement and then being able to drill into that detail.

The account analysis system should **NOT** demand input files contain specific service code values. Demanding specific service codes puts unnecessary constraints on data file providers / senders (third party vendors). Best practice would allow a sender to use any service code they want for a file. The account analysis system should make it as easy as possible for the sender of service billing data by providing needed translation capabilities.

For this reason, it is best practice for account analysis to support both an internal service code and an external service code. Service volumes enter the analysis system with *external* service codes. Service Code **ABCD1234** above for example is considered an external code, because *Paid Checks* within the analysis system might be *Analysis Service Code* 0020. The posting process then, simply needs to know that external Service Code **ABCD1234** should accumulate under internal *Analysis Service Code 0020.*

Supporting this lookup during posting of a file, means senders / vendors can use any code(s) they want, because the analysis system should be able to interpret what is being sent and where to post it. Time has shown that sometimes two different File Types (ACH and RDC departments for example) might both have an external code **ABCD1234** on them, but they mean different things. For this reason, the best practice would be that for any service code translation, it should be based on the type of file (File Type ID) from which a transaction originated.

> *Some analysis systems support the concept of service code translation, but it isn't always by file type. Some systems will look at any Service Code ABCD1234 (no matter where it came from) and turn it into internal code 0020 if that is the how the translation is set up. In the real world, Service Code ABCD1234 on an RDC file might mean something entirely different than Service Code ABCD1234 on an ACH File.*

When dealing with many external billing files, having a file catalogue (or library) is helpful to operations in numerous ways. Imagine an operations unit responsible for processing 27 different billing files. Below is a sample of a file catalog with just a few files shown.

In my opinion, each file entry should support an underlying File Type (a detailed description of the file content), and the services typically gathered from the file. The catalogue would normally be built during an implementation project and then serve as valuable documentation while the system lives in production.

As time passes, certain files will no longer be used, and new file types will certainly be introduced. A small bank would likely only have about 5 to 10 catalogue entries while a large bank could easily have over 100 entries in the file definition catalogue.

File Type ID	Source	Description	Date Usage Started	Expected Recurrance	Date Usage Ended
1	ACH	ACH Origination Billing File - ACH Traker	Jun-25	Monthly	-
2	RDC	Image Center Billing File	Jun-25	Monthly	-
3	POS	Positive Pay Billing File	Jun-25	Monthly	-
4	DDA	Deposit System Core Interface File (IBS)	Jun-25	Daily	-

Best practice is for data files to be picked up automatically by any posting system and the file definition catalogue is then used to identify each file (likely by a file name pattern). Once a file is identified it can be added to what would be called a Monthly Processing File Catalogue.

When a file is added to the Monthly File Processing Catalogue, a File ID is assigned so when the input records are processed, they can be associated to the original source file (and easily eliminated from a monthly process if / when needed).

Monthly File Processing Catalog

File ID	Server File Name	Date Posted	Source	Description (Click to See Posting Report)	Input Records
1	\\ServerName\	6/1/2025	ACH	ACH Origination Billing File - ACH Tracker	1,112
2	\\ServerName\	6/1/2025	RDC	Image Center Billing File	532
3	\\ServerName\	6/1/2025	POS	Positive Pay Billing File	498
4	\\ServerName\	6/1/2025	DDA	Deposit System Core Interface File (IBS)	4,609

Integration of Billing Data

Because account analysis is a billing system supporting billing data from all over the bank and from 3rd party vendors, the data collection process needs to be powerful in the handling of disparate formats. History shows that there will always be *new* service billing files from 3rd party vendors. Vendors (and their billing files) come and go through time, so the support for ease of integration is imperative. For many years past, a new service billing file meant a need for another interface program of some sort to handle the translation and formatting of data.

A best practice for data integration would be for the account analysis system to include a data mapping and translation tool where a focus is placed on simplicity and ease of use. A tool like this processes input data using meta data to describe inputs. In the end, banks familiar with account analysis want to know they can easily ingest billing data into their billing system, without designing and writing entire programs to do so.

Standing Files

Sometimes an account analysis department is left with billing data that needs to be processed, but there is no billing file from a 3rd party vendor. I often tell FI's that when selecting 3rd party vendors to deal with, make sure that the vendor commits to providing a billing file at least monthly so that the fees being charged to a bank can easily be passed on to the accounts responsible for the fees in the first place.

Without a monthly billing file, an operations department is often faced with manual data entry and / or simply not processing the billing information from the vendor at all (thus creating yet more ROL-Revenue Opportunity Lost).

A middle ground between complete automation and manual data entry is used by many FI's. This middle ground is something I refer to as a standing file. Imagine an invoice of some sort from a 3rd party vendor containing account information and charges being passed to an FI. These monthly invoices often look very much the same from month to month and often contain the same accounts, the same or similar volumes/charges, and the same services.

Most analysis systems support the concept of uploading a spreadsheet of some sort containing such billing data. What if analysis operations were to create a standing spreadsheet (once) with all the customers (and their deposit account numbers) and the volume / charge for the month. While it still involves manual intervention, a person could easily scan the monthly invoice and compare it to the normal / standard volume / charge on the standing spreadsheet making any necessary edits. At the completion of the visual scan (including the possibility of adding / removing customers) an operations person could simply upload the standing spreadsheet and create the necessary billing entries.

While not the most ideal, this technique is a tremendous improvement over an operations department simply tossing the billing aside. Once implemented, an analysis operations person will soon find that the data entry requirements for such a procedure are minimal, as 90% of what the analysis system needs (account numbers, service codes, etc.) is already there.

Process & Procedures

I cannot begin to describe the amount of time and effort over the years put into the development of controls surrounding commercial billing error prevention. One of the first controls ever developed dealt with volume reason-ability limits. A warning message would be shown on any account where a posted volume seemed unreasonable for the line-item service in question. Let's face it, a small business should not have a charge for 10 Stop Payment Orders for a given month. While valuable, volume reasonability controls lose their luster when one realizes that 10 Stop Payment Orders for a given month would be perfectly normal for very large business clients. With more advanced systems, this differentiation has led to volume reason-ability controls by account type.

While volumes may take center stage for monitoring (and issuing warning messages) rates, factors, and even important status settings have also caught the attention of input controls. An earnings credit rate of 10% would be unreasonable in any bank. A *Check Printing Charge* of $1,321 (which probably should have been $13.21) would certainly create a warning. How about status codes where an account is to be W-Waived for a specified number of months? It wouldn't be reasonable to Waive an account for 30 months. The input intent in this case would more likely be 3.0 months.

These examples are all "errors of commission" where a person (or system) did something whether intentional or not, that resulted in an incorrect value being entered or processed. Sometimes these errors result in data not being allowed/posted into a system in the first place (like a 30-month waiver). Other times erroneous data makes it into a system and creates an unusually high service charge, causing contention for the end customer paying the bill.

While input controls described here help make the FI's account analysis process more accurate, I have most recently grasped onto something that appears to be much more costly to financial institutions. The commercial billing problem financial institutions should be laser focused on is not errors of commission, but errors of omission.

By turning the focus to end results of account analysis vs. placing control land mines across the fields of input processing, one will find the most expensive billing errors of all in commercial billing. Have you ever looked at a statement and wondered why is there a charge for ACH Originated Items but no line-item charge for ACH Origination Maintenance? How about charges for Online Outgoing Wires but no line-item fee for using the Online Wire Transfer Module in the first place?

ACH and Wires don't have the market cornered on these missing maintenance fees. They are also missing from Lock Box, Remote Deposit Capture, Account Recon, and other Positive Pay / Fraud Prevention Services. In fact, any time a billing blueprint of services contains product families where there are monthly maintenance fees and associated item fees, there is a very high degree of probability that there are missing service fees. Very unlike the errors of commission, these errors largely go unnoticed even though they are punching FI revenue right in the face. Customers certainly aren't going to call their bank to complain about these types of errors. Who has time to search all the statements for such anomalies? Across the account base, how many accounts and services might be affected by these errors of omission? When unit prices are considered and applied, what dollar value do these errors all add up to for a single month?

In some financial institutions, the problem goes beyond maintenance fees. Wouldn't you think that if an account has charges for ACH Originated Items there would also be some sort of charge for ACH Originated Files of Batches? Every financial institution could derive business rules simply by looking at the blueprint of line-item services in their commercial billing. I like to refer to this as *Rules Based Logic* (and the rules would be different at every institution). Inverse rules could also be a part of an FI's Rules Based Logic. For example, if an account is charged for ARP Maintenance each month one would expect to see a line-item charge somewhere on the statement for *ARP Issued Items* or perhaps *ARP Paid Items*.

Explaining *why* there are billing gaps like described here is not easy. The origin of these problems has a lot to do with conversions, mergers and acquisitions, new systems, new products, new versions of existing systems and/or products, human errors, procedural errors, and workflow errors. Best practice would be to find and sweep up all the errors of omission but also to try and understand the source so that the problem(s) don't' reappear or become larger.

All these errors contribute to something I refer to as ROL-Revenue Opportunity Lost. Within account analysis there are many factors that contribute to an FI's total ROL. I feel compelled to sub-categorize errors of omission as e-ROL where the "e" stands for *erroneous* (and in some cases embarrassing). I would go as far as saying that "NOT establishing an internal project at some point to seek out all e-ROL in an FI's commercial billing system may in fact be, an FI's largest error of omission".

Preliminary Analysis

Most commercial banks will begin the operationally arduous monthly billing process by launching a preliminary analysis. As is true for other steps in the monthly analysis process, best practice is for this preliminary generation of analysis results to be scheduled and executed automatically. There shouldn't be a requirement for back-office users to remember to execute this step or need to push buttons causing the process to be launched.

This said, a preliminary generation of analysis should only be performed once the bulk of all billing data has been collected in account analysis. Once preliminary results are generated there will be a validation process. It simply doesn't make sense to start the validation process when we already know there are significant amounts of data still missing.

The final data feed from the demand deposit system (for the month) certainly would be one constraint an FI would want to consider before doing a preliminary analysis. Ancillary systems like Wires, ACH, RDC, Positive Pay, etc. will also have a significant amount of data that an FI will want to be included in the preliminary analysis. Traditionally, Lockbox billing files often arrive several days after a month is closed. There isn't a strong need to wait for the Lockbox Files(s). These files typically affect few accounts so one can make good use of time to launch the preliminary analysis even before the arrival of final files like this, so that the validation process can begin.

The best practice in validating the preliminary analysis is to focus on the line item services across the entire bank. Volumes from month to month should be reasonable, as should the gross fees calculated. The concept is simple really, if the months gone by have been accurate and we are in the same range with volumes and fees as months gone by, one can feel rather confident that the preliminary analysis is well within the guardrails of accuracy. Total fees to be debited, invoiced, referred, etc. should all be within good reason before making the decision to close out the month.

> *The validation process in account analysis reminds me of an old cliché which became very popular back in the 70's. It went something like this: "To error is human, to really foul things up, requires a computer".*

The End of Month Close Process

Closing out the month for analysis typically happens after all the results have been verified. The process involves creating the final statements for distribution, creating debits for all fees that are due, creating credits for any interest amounts being paid, creating a data warehouse file for passing all results to downstream systems, and sometimes more. Closing the month in most commercial banks happens by the middle of the calendar month following the actual month being processed.

Best practice is for the end of month close process to be scheduled by operations and then to have it be executed automatically based upon this scheduling. Scheduling of course sometimes needs to be modified. The objective is for a process like this to happen via automation vs. back-office users pushing buttons for each task to be done.

As stated, this end of month close process creates debits to be processed by the core deposit system. When the debit transactions are processed, they will be reducing the deposit balances in all the business accounts on file. This major step in the monthly analysis process is sometimes cause for contentiousness.

Softening the Blow of Automatic Debits

When you think about it, the automatic debiting that is done in commercial account analysis is about the only automatic payment performed in all of banking, that a customer does not intentionally sign up for.

If that isn't bizarre enough, how about the fact that the amount of the automatic payment changes each month, so a customer has little to no idea as to how much the charge is going to be, until it happens. While this traditional automatic debiting is considered normal for anyone involved with treasury management billing, it can often contribute to what may unnecessarily become a confrontational relationship between a bank and a bank's business customer.

The concept of a bank review, followed by a customer review before the automatic debit (which requires a debit-delay period) can soften the blow of such service charging, especially when there is some sort of error involved in the monthly fees. Properly handled, this approach allows a month to be completely finalized, billing statements to be produced and delivered (however a bank chooses) and only after a customer has had a chance to review the billing statement, does an automatic debit process take place.

Now of course the number of days for reviewing (and delaying the auto-debit) may vary, based upon the type of customer. A non-analyzed (fee-based) small business account billing is rather easy to understand so a short 4-day delay is likely all that is needed. A bank's most sophisticated customers are often more complex (and more important) when it comes to commercial billing so a longer bank review and debit delay (the time for customer review) may be appropriate to allow more time.

Whatever the case, one size here surely does not fit all. For larger institutions and account volumes, I would suggest the answer is *Multi-*

ple Settlement Cycles. Using multiple cycles, a bank operations team can move the non-analyzed accounts quickly through the monthly billing process while reserving more review time for the bank's larger commercial customers.

To keep treasury operations at the bank happy, I think the clincher to implementing a plan like this is to make sure that any changes to an account (between the date of statement delivery and the planned day of the auto-debit) must automatically regenerate the results for the account / relationship. Before the end of a delay period then, any changes to results need to automatically change the debit amount on its' way to the core deposit system (and likely send a corrected statement as well).

I think this approach takes some of the confrontation out of a customer relationship yet keeps the entire process as automated as possible. I would suggest that proactive planning steps like these will reduce the constant need for *reactive* adjustments due to errors in account analysis.

Nine

Treasury Management Sales

Opportunity Identification

If you have ever glanced at an Account Analysis statement you might have found the complexity to be a bit intimidating. Let's face it, terms like "Collected Balance Required" and "Non-Compensable Services" are not terms we hear every day. There is no wonder why the AFP sponsors annual educational sessions on decoding account analysis statements at their national conference. If you were to take some time to see through the complexity of this monthly report (which is what an account analysis statement really is), you would be surprised to find that you can discover a tremendous amount of information about a business customer.

It is important to first understand that all the information on the account analysis report is collected and brought together from several different areas within a bank. This gathering of information repeats itself every month. Once this information is all collected and presented, anyone looking at the report will get to see all the activity for the customer. Imagine, existing processes within every bank with commercial accounts are already gathering and collecting information on business accounts, bringing it all together, sorting it into a logical and presentable fashion, and then making the entire report available to those who care to see it.

Service fees related to ACH Origination, Wire Transfer, Lockbox, etc. all originate in these various departments of a bank and typically are shown in separate sections of an analysis statement. These sections are often referred to as product categories. These product categories typically have several services within them. Visualize a small business customer that is being charged a service fee for 2 International Wire Transfers. A single service like this on an analysis report would certainly make you wonder what sort of business this customer is running. Most billing system vendors make this analysis data available for month over month review. Would it mean anything if the International Wire Transfers showing up on the statement have never been seen before? Or if they happen to be on the statement every month? What can you learn from a statement where the customer is being charged for 637 Paid Checks this month? Does the same statement show any fees for a Check Positive Pay service? Such a situation might point to an opportunity to sell the customer on the idea of a Positive Pay Service.

Suffice to say that analysis statements show us what a customer is doing, but they also show us what a customer is not doing. Developing service correlations then can lead to direct hits in terms of sales leads. A customer with many deposited items but no evidence of RDC-Remote Deposit Capture usage, clearly seems to be a candidate for RDC. The analysis statement can also show customer anomalies as well. What if a statement showed a monthly recurring fee for Remote Deposit Capture but there were not any RDC Item fees on the statement? Could it be the customer is not using their RDC Service? What if a customer had a subscription fee for Online Banking on the statement but is choosing to do wires manually at the branch instead? Would it be of value to know exactly who these customers are?

Customer activity is highlighted within each of the treasury management products being used. I am not sure there is better document that could help a bank with knowing more about their customers. While KYC may be a mandate in the industry, from a treasury management sales perspective the analysis statement should be the driving force behind KYO (Know Your Opportunity).

Given an account analysis system with basic customer information display capabilities, a TM salesperson can learn quite a bit regarding a customer in advance of meeting with them. In a worst-case scenario, one could review each of the individual analysis statements for a customer by pulling them up one by one. The best practice would be to have an analysis *Trend* view of the statement data so that a user could in effect, see a whole year worth of statements on a single trend view screen.

Confirming Concession Pricing

One of my favorite expressions is "you don't get a second chance to make a first impression". As a TM salesperson who just sold a customer products / services and made pricing concessions in the process, it is very important to review the preliminary analysis statements for the customer to make certain that all concession pricing made it into the onboarding of the account. If you are the salesperson who convinced the customer to buy such services, it is entirely up to you to ensure the pricing is correct. Nobody else in the bank is going to care as much as the TM salesperson must care about the accuracy of all the approved concession pricing.

The account analysis system and the preliminary analysis process must allow for an officer review of the preliminary statements before charges are finalized. Most commercial banks are finalizing their account analysis by the 15th calendar day of the month (for balances and activity of the previous month). The best practice includes a notification to all treasury sales officers that the preliminary analysis is complete, and it is time for them to log into the system and review the preliminary statements.

Treasury salespeople will often say they do not have time to review all their accounts / statements for accuracy. I say that all new customer relationships need to be reviewed because that is where the highest potential for error exists. Once a customer is on the system and all the pricing is set, the only on-going concern would be an unusually large volume or something creating a large variance. Pricing problems normally happen during an onboarding process and that is where an account review is most important.

I will add that customers with extremely large volumes / total fees due each month should be reviewed as well. These customers are amongst the most important of all customers in the bank. A quick review of the fees due and the reasonability surrounding such is well worth the effort if you are the relationship manager assigned to such account(s).

Account Modeling

What if a bank could enter estimated service volumes, balances, and their current pricing into a highly sophisticated calculator so everyone involved could visualize the results of such analysis? This is essentially what account modeling is. A treasury salesperson / analyst could see revenue possibilities generated through such an exercise. In addition to revenue, most modeling tools would also calculate and display the profitability of any modeling scenario.

Some modeling tools only calculate marginal profitability based upon the price and cost of each line-item service. More sophisticated modeling tools support more advanced calculations such as the concept of indirect costs, which are surcharges for an entire product category. The concept of applying a yield rate to an account balance (aka. funds transfer pricing) is also considered to be a more advanced feature in an account analysis modeling tool. Applying a yield rate to a customer balance would show that an account with a very large balance might be more profitable to a bank than an account with substantial transaction activity.

The end goal for the bank is to identify everything involved regarding an opportunity including not just the potential revenue, but also the costs involved, the resulting margin (dollars and percent), the pricing realization (how close is the model to list pricing?), and even the revenue opportunity lost with any such model. Simply said, account modeling is "what if?" analysis, or as I often say, "let's see how deep that puddle is before we step into it".

> *A small community bank on the Kentucky side of the Ohio River, just across from the city of Cincinnati, once signed what they thought was the "deal of the century". When the bank landed a lockbox agreement for the largest telephone company in the region, there were celebrations beyond anything I'd ever seen in an office environment. As time went on, everyone learned of the tremendous costs involved for the new lockbox operation. Costs included hardware, software, and even new real estate required to house the new equipment. The wonderful lockbox opportunity the bank thought they had won turned into one of the costliest operations ever. The telephone company soon became the bank's loss leader.*

Using Excel

For many years, the concept of building proformas for modeling purposes was mostly done in Excel. Even today, there are Excel modeling templates widely used to measure the profitability of a given relationship based upon proposed pricing, service costs, and balances. Some refer to this process as *deal (or offer) management*. As time has passed, the use of Excel to handle this function has exposed several flaws, not the least of which is making sure the Excel templates have all the current products / services as well as up to date pricing.

Another problem born from the Excel approach is trying to implement a workflow approval process for a modeling proposal. Using Excel workbooks, the proforma's end up attached to emails and multiple versions of them end up all over the place. Perhaps the most significant problem with using Excel for proforma modeling is the need for eventual concession pricing to be re-entered into the actual account analysis system once approved.

CRM and Other External Tools

Through the years, there have been attempts to build external modeling systems that stand alone outside the core account analysis billing system. These attempts have struggled at best, with having all the needed data to perform proforma creation. It is not as simple as having access to the current products and services for all standard pricing at a bank. Different account analysis systems have unique approaches to defining and applying bank standards (aka. LIST) pricing.

One approach to LIST pricing is to have the analysis system define all the products and services in a bank standard table established for such. Banks often though have different standards for different accounts. Sometimes it has to do with the account type (e.g. small business vs. large corporate customer) or even the demographics of the account (e.g. cost center, region, etc.).

Some systems establish these alternative standards with a secondary table of standards to override the default LIST price. Other systems use price LISTS that layer over the top of one another based upon a hierarchical priority established by the bank.

Stand-alone modeling tools are then faced with the impossible task of making use of such LIST pricing because each bank's analysis system treats standard LIST pricing tables in such unique ways. Developing external modeling tools like this require complex / custom programming and development for integration into any bank's account analysis system. The only alternative would be redundant pricing tables being maintained, which nobody wants.

The need for modeling tools in account analysis goes well beyond new account prospects too. Banks also need the intrinsic ability to model existing account pricing concessions after time goes by, when renewal dates arrive. Attempting to build any external modeling application means feeding any such tool with all the banks standard pricing as well as all the bank's account information, the existing account concessions, and even the entire account data store just to create a model for an existing account.

There have been attempts to implement external modeling functionality into CRM systems. While some CRM systems now have limited or basic modeling capability for new prospects, they typically don't have the necessary account information to evaluate existing pricing concessions, making such modeling weak at best.

The absolute best practice for the creation of modeling proformas for account analysis is to have any/all modeling functionality embedded within the account analysis system itself. Using this approach, access to LIST pricing is well understood and products / pricing for all treasury management services are updated in real time. Any concession pricing for completed / approved models is then easily applied to the analysis system.

The Workflow Approval Process

When using Excel for modeling as so many banks do, the workflow approval process typically involves emailing a workbook amongst co-workers and eventually coming to a consensus on pricing. Any deviation from standard pricing is then re-entered into the account analysis system.

More advanced account analysis solutions have implemented a value-based workflow approval process. This means that the overall value of the concession being made will define the number and level of approvals required for eventual approval. After all, a 100% discount for an entire customer relationship should be a more difficult approval process than simply reducing account fees by 10%. To evaluate the value of any/all concessions, approvers need access to important metrics like price realization, margin, variance, and revenue opportunity lost, all of which are intrinsic to the analysis system calculations.

The best practice for an automated workflow approval process is that it too, live within the account analysis system itself. The key performance indicators mentioned above involve comparisons to LIST price, which itself can be a very complex factor to arrive at in any modeling evaluation.

Workflow Challenges

One challenge with any workflow approval process in treasury modeling is that senior level people who need to approve pricing proposals (e.g. sales management) often do not want to log into an analysis system to do the approvals. A single sign on to the account analysis system can alleviate some of the anguish, especially when the modeling system takes one right to the model that needs approving. For senior management not wanting to sign into a workflow for approvals, a communication delegate for the approver, can sometimes bridge the gap.

Modeling Complexity

Through time, many banks have complained about too much complexity in modeling. The complexity comes from the modeling tools attempting to cover every possible situation imaginable and displaying them all on a single screen. Most often, proforma modeling involves analyzing a service volume at a unit price vs. the bank's standard unit (LIST) price for the service.

In environments where I've seen the modeling tools used successfully, I have found that the bank identified 2 or 3 staff members to take responsibility for model / proforma creation. Treasury salespeople should be out talking with potential customers and selling. They cannot get bogged down by the intricacies of a fee-based service vs. a compensable service.

If a bank has a few proforma wizards that can get the details from a salesperson and produce a modeling proforma on the behalf of the salesperson, it is much more effective use of everyone's time. The best practice is to not try and force modeling tools down the throat of every salesperson. It is best to have a sales operations person / team handle this phase of winning new business.

Concession Pricing Life Cycle Management

Treasury Management sales officers are very much a part of concession pricing in account analysis. Best practice is to always have an expiration date on any pricing concession. The expiration date becomes a review date in effect and ensures that concession pricing doesn't fly under the radar or far into the future.

Best practices include the account analysis system seeing an expiration date approaching and then alerting the treasury sales officer of the impending concession expiration. Done properly, a sales officer could easily just allow the expiration to occur or instead, create a new modeling proforma using historical data for the customer. The new proforma would show the concession pricing currently in effect but also make it easy for a sales team analyst to suggest new pricing (I often refer to this as *clawing back* on concession pricing). Once such a model is submitted for approval, the expiration dates would eventually be updated, and the account alerts would stop until it is time for the next renewal cycle.

Managing all of this within the analysis system provides enhanced automation, less manual effort, and improved accuracy as customers go through a pricing review process.

Ten

Product Management

Measuring Lift from Repricing Events

The arduous chore of repricing treasury management services in commercial banks often results in an even more difficult task of measuring the success from such efforts. Assume for a moment that the goal of repricing products and services is to enhance top line revenue whether it be through organic growth or through winning over new customers. The repricing effort takes time, research, and collaboration. Once new pricing is implemented though, how does a financial institution go about measuring the success of such efforts? Were the decisions made during repricing process the correct decisions? It is not a simple *Yes* or *No* answer. The question needs to be broken down into multiple questions for analysis, where the sum of the answers reflects the actual level of success.

The first thing one will need to successfully measure repricing performance / revenue lift is existing KPI's (key performance indicators). For example, how many non-analyzed small business accounts were opened in the 12 months preceding the repricing event? Having this KPI on hand makes it possible to compare to the number of newly opened small business accounts after the repricing event. If prices have been set too high for example, the bank is likely to find a reduction in new accounts opened. The same KPI should be measured for single / stand-alone analyzed accounts and analyzed composite relationships (a single customer with 2+ deposit accounts linked together). Having this granular level of information would show the bank they might be successful with a certain type of account while not so successful with another. The very same KPI's should be tracked for accounts leaving the bank (closed accounts) because if repricing is too invasive, customer's will pack up their balances and leave the bank.

Having the KPI's stated above will provide reasoning for changes in top line revenue (total fees due before any earnings credit allowance). The top line revenue needs to be tracked separately for existing customers (before repricing) and new customers that opened accounts after the repricing event went into effect. There needs to be a special focus on the existing customers because what can happen is those customers will balk at the new unit pricing and demand that their pricing not change at all even though bank standard pricing is changing. In cases like this, account level pricing exceptions are often built to maintain the current account pricing and bypass the repricing event all together. The irony in this circumstance is that while the original intent was to grow revenue, instead the bank has gone to much effort only to grow their internal expense.

Knowing that non-interest income will increase with new accounts and decrease with closed accounts, the associated revenue from these categories needs to be isolated so that one can gain insight into what is happening with fee income across the portfolio of long-term existing customers. A variance in trends for new or closed accounts could directly be attributable to the repricing event itself (good or bad). If there is consistency over time with both new and closed accounts, one may have to look deeper into line-item services to understand revenue variance from long term customers. For example, are clients starting to use

Same Day ACH services more now due to the new price of Domestic Wires? Were either of these services included in the repricing event?

It is entirely possible that a repricing event for one product could be considered successful while poor decisions were made regarding the repricing of another product. To circumvent such, it might make sense for a bank to conduct repricing events for one product at a time. Measuring the success of a repricing event will be more accurate if all the changes are attributable to a single product family. In this scenario a bank might consider repricing events to be ongoing with 6-month time slots of success measurement. If all Wire Transfer services are repriced and no other products are repriced at the same time, one could do a rather accurate analysis of the effect of repricing the Wire Services product.

Repricing of ACH Origination Services then, should likely not begin until the Wire Services analysis is complete. In this way, bank management will gain better insight into the overall effect of pricing changes by product vs. just changing the price of everything at once. This more granular approach to repricing products will ultimately lead to more accuracy into decisions made over time, especially when a product like Wires needs to be repriced again.

Essential to any repricing process is a repricing analysis tool that measures customer impact in advance of repricing implementation. A modeling tool such as this allows product management to understand what impact their decisions are likely to have on banking customers. I always like to say, "let's see how deep this puddle is before we step into it". Product level modeling will allow for success prediction when it comes to repricing, but it cannot guarantee success. Real success requires an accurate accounting of KPI's and then the results of those measurements to be favorable to the bank. For example, did the bank open more accounts after the repricing event? Did fewer accounts (than normal) close? Is there an actual revenue lift among the existing long-term customers?

To be sure, the success measurement process can be a slippery slope. My suggestion would be to start on the "bunny hill" and work your way up. The bumps and bruises from falls along the way will have you mastering the black diamond level in no time.

Multicurrency Handling in Account Analysis

The concept of an earnings credit allowance being applied to offset treasury management fees for customers was born in the United States, and it all started with the enactment of Regulation Q back in 1933, a regulation which prohibited the payment of interest on checking accounts. As such, most account analysis systems in use today were initially developed as single currency systems with all amounts based on USD.

> *Still today, the concept of applying an earnings credit allowance to bank fees due, is not generally seen outside of the US.*

Automatic debiting or billing for banking services however is a practice that has no borders. Standards for Bank Services Billing (BSB) were developed by the TWIST organization long ago to assist with bank fee monitoring internationally, where multiple currencies had to be supported well beyond the single currency systems in the US.

Once ISO assumed ownership of the modified TWIST BSB Standard and the AFP developed a new set of common, global service codes, a new global electronic statement standard known as the "camt.086" evolved. The detailed specifications for "camt.086" included currency codes for balances, service pricing, compensation, and taxation. This meant that a multicurrency billing system would not only need to support multiple currencies amongst accounts, but that such a system would also need to support multiple currencies within a single account.

Account Analysis Currency Codes

Because the global standard for bank services billing is now well documented and widely adopted, any account analysis system claiming to be a *multicurrency* system would need to include currency codes throughout the application. Done properly, a multicurrency account analysis system would align with the new global standards, more specifically to the following components of account analysis:

-**Balances**: This is the currency of the account as held in the deposit system or "feeder" application. Balances in account analysis are maintained (stored or displayed) in the account's *Balance Currency*. The *Balance Currency* code is typically stored at the account level and/or defaulted from a higher level in the system's data structure.

-**Compensation / Settlement:** This is the currency in which the billing relationship would be charged and/or settled. In most cases, a direct debit in this currency would be created to collect service charges from the customer account. Any earnings allowance from analysis would also be maintained in this *Settlement Currency,* as would and any excess / deficit amounts shown in the compensation section of the analysis statement. The *Settlement Currency* code is typically stored at the account level and/or defaulted from a higher level in the system's data structure.

-**Pricing**: This is the currency used to price a single service and in which service charges are accumulated. The service *Pricing Currency* would typically be specified at the line-item service level but likely would default from a higher level in the system's data structure. While all services would likely be in a single *Pricing Currency*, a premium multicurrency system would support the concept of a single line-item service being specified in a different *Pricing Currency* from the rest.

-**Taxation:** Taxes on treasury management services is not widespread in the US but is an essential component of bank services billing internationally. Taxing authorities receiving payments from banks (for banking services provided), receive such in a *Host* Currency. In a multicurrency analysis system, taxes are converted from the *Pricing Currency* to the *Host Currency* when calculating tax payments. The total tax amount is converted to the *Settlement Currency* when collecting taxes from a customer and stipulating such in the Compensation Section of an analysis statement.

Multicurrency Translations

Any multicurrency system needs to deal with currency translations and account analysis is no exception. Currency translation in account analysis happens between components on a single statement, in the aggregation of multiple accounts in a multi-account relationship, and in reporting across the portfolio of all accounts on analysis.

Currency translation is based upon foreign exchange rates, so it is imperative that a multicurrency account analysis system have access to such rates. An earnings allowance rate in account analysis is typically applied to account balances covering an entire month. One approach to stipulating foreign exchange rates would be to handle them just as ECR rates are handled, typically planted into the account analysis system for reference. Using this approach, every translation imaginable would have to be stipulated within the system and maintained.

Another approach to foreign exchange rates would be an analysis system making an external call (an API) to a service providing exchange rates as of a specific date/time along with from and to currency codes. Regardless of approach, a currency translation cannot occur without a rate so exchange rates (and how they are accessed) are a very important element of any multicurrency analysis system.

Multicurrency Account Analysis Statements

Each component of a multicurrency account analysis statement would / should have a currency type code associated with it. An *Average Ledger Balance* for example, is an element that would be assigned to the *Balance Currency* type. For example, if the *Balance Currency* is set to NZD for an account, one would assume the entire balance section of the account analysis statement to be in NZD-New Zealand Dollars. In this case, any input file presenting balance information for an account with a Balance Currency of NZD, would/should also be in New Zealand dollars.

An earnings credit allowance on the other hand, is an element that lives within the Compensation / Settlement component of the analysis statement. Calculation and display for earnings credit then, are done in the *Settlement Currency* of the account. Each section of a multicurrency account analysis statement should reflect the correct currency code used for the statement component.

> *While an earnings credit rate is in the compensation section of an account analysis statement, the earnings rate itself would not be linked to a specific currency code. Whether 3% of GBP or 3% of CAN, it is simply 3%. For percentage rates in account analysis, there is no rate conversion.*

With multiple currencies, comes multiple currency symbols. Any use of currency symbols on analysis statements should reflect the correct currency symbol for the currency being used ($, €, £, etc.).

Multicurrency Account Analysis Relationships

Some account analysis systems claiming to be *multicurrency* systems have many built in limitations. Anyone digging into multicurrency capabilities would have to do a deep dive to understand what those limitations are. In the case of account relationships, some analysis systems would require that all subsidiary accounts within a relationship of accounts, be in the same currency. Not only would all components of a statement (balances, settlement, etc.) need to be in the same currency but all subsidiary accounts within the relationship would also have to be in the same currency. This limitation occurs when an analysis system has no currency translation between components of the account analysis statement or in the aggregation of analysis accounts altogether.

A premium multicurrency account analysis system would allow for currency translations within an account and across all accounts within a relationship. Given three accounts using three different currencies for balances, the relationship summary account would be the target for currency translation. Detail account balances in this case, would be converted and aggregated into the relationship summary account balance currency type for display on the account analysis statement.

Multicurrency Reporting in Account Analysis

When I think of reporting in account analysis across the entire portfolio of accounts, I don't generally think of what currency a specific account may be using. If I wanted to see a *Debit & Invoice Register* of all accounts for example, I would want all accounts to be reflected on the report. Some analysis systems would require a user to run such a report only for accounts using a specific currency code. The reason is the same as the weaknesses of a system requiring all accounts of an account relationship to be in the same currency, that being there is no currency translation within.

When it comes to report setup and design, a user should be able to stipulate what target currency is to be used in the generation of the report. Any report out of the system should have a target currency. If a user wanted to see a Debit & Invoice Register in USD, then any account with a non-USD *Settlement Currency* would have to convert the debit amount to USD for display on the report.

This currency translation activity is very similar to having an account relationship using multiple currencies amongst the subsidiary accounts. Any account using a currency code that is different than the relationship parent currency target, must have the amount(s) translated using foreign exchange rates.

Imagine having a report in any target currency where the report includes all accounts for the bank, regardless of their specific currency code. Using currency code itself as a report filter, would also support the concept of creating certain reports for accounts with specific currency codes.

Multicurrency Account Analysis Summary

When evaluating the capabilities of an account analysis system, it isn't as easy as checking the box for multicurrency support. The new global standard for account analysis reporting "camt.086" is an excellent guide for the detailed components of what a premium multicurrency account analysis system looks like. Currency translation / foreign exchange is required for account analysis and it involves the components of a statement for a single account, aggregation of data across multiple accounts, and most certainly in the creation of reports for an entire portfolio in a target currency.

Eleven

Account Analysis Reporting

Some of the best account analysis reporting for a bank can come from account analysis data contained in the bank's data warehouse. One of the tremendous advantages of using a data warehouse for reporting is that even though vendor systems come and go, the data warehouse data-store remains.

During an account analysis implementation project at a large regional bank in Texas, I was informed the system being implemented needed to feed the bank's data warehouse for reporting purposes. I initially argued that the system being installed could provide some of the reporting already being generated by the data warehouse. What I learned in the process was that the reporting out of the data warehouse was not being changed at all, only the host billing system was changing.

As it turned out, the bank was continuing to use a very consistent set of standard reports and graphs based upon account analysis information. In fact, this was the 3rd analysis system being implemented in 10 years at the bank, but the data warehouse reporting of revenue and expense had never changed.

When management within the bank looked at the monthly reporting of treasury management accounts, products, and services they had no idea the bank had even converted to an entirely new analysis system.

It was during this implementation project that I learned the true value of a bank's data warehouse.

In this chapter, I will cover some of the basic reporting that could be created for account analysis. The suggested reporting is separated by the role a user has, so the data-views described below pertain to Operations, Product Management, and Sales Management.

Operational Reporting

Some of the most useful reports or data-views for the operations team are anything that illustrates change. The operations department working on account analysis is mostly concerned with what has changed, what is different, and what variances exist this month as compared to previous months gone by.

While Product Management & Sales Management Reporting are mostly focused on the finalized results of analysis, operational reporting is more focused on preliminary results which offer users an opportunity to correct whatever may be wrong, before the finalized results are produced.

Variance reporting is of great concern to operations. Best practices involve starting with variances to volumes. The reason for this is that volumes are the most fluid part of account analysis calculations each month. While pricing certainly goes through change in account analysis, it is the volumes from the billing process that are naturally different each month from every input known to the system. The question here becomes how different are they? Are they so different that we may have missed an entire input file? Are they so different that we may have double posted an input file? The answer comes down to variance and understanding the volume variance and tolerance thresholds.

Volume Variance by Product Group – Current Month

One of the best practices in operations is to always make use of a Volume Variance Report each month. A variance report like this is generally not focused on service charges but instead, the service volume for each line-item service within each product category.

Volume Variance by Product Category - March 2025

Product Family	*Bank Service ID Code*	*Description*	*Nov-24 Final*	*Dec-24 Final*	*Jan-25 Final*	*Feb-25 Prelim*	*Volume Variance*	*Variance %*	*Average*
		*** Depository Services**							
DEP	1001	Deposits Posted – Paper	16	18	19	19	-	-	18
DEP	1002	Deposited Items	41	36	33	31	(2)	-6%	37
DEP	1003	Debits Posted – Paper	35	37	32	32	-	-	35
DEP	1004	Debits Posted – Electronic	4	2	2	2	-	-	3
DEP	1005	Deposit Correction	2	1	1	1	-	-	1
DEP	1007	Stop Payment	2,106	1,984	2,082	1,443	(639)	-31%	2,057
DEP	1009	Check Copies	2	1	1	2	1	100%	1
		*** ACH Origination Services**							
ACH	2504	ACH Per/File Originated	5	3	4	3	(1)	-25%	4
ACH	2505	ACH Debit Block	5,423	5,670	5,940	4,050	(1,890)	-32%	5,678
ACH	2506	ACH File Reversal	156	147	154	140	(14)	-9%	152
ACH	2507	ACH Origination File Repair	27	25	26	29	3	12%	26
ACH	2508	ACH Returns	323	348	350	350	-	-	340
ACH	2509	ACH NOCs	69	66	72	74	2	3%	69
ACH	2510	ACH Debits and Credits	21	18	19	20	1	5%	19
		*** Wire Transfer Services**							
WIR	3503	Wire Notification – eMail	12	13	15	15	-	-	13
WIR	3504	Wire Notification – Phone	23	20	22	46	24	109%	22
WIR	3505	Outgoing International Wire	17	15	16	18	2	13%	16
WIR	3506	Incoming International Wire	8	9	10	11	1	10%	9
WIR	3507	Outgoing Domestic Wire	7	6	6	7	1	17%	6
WIR	3508	Incoming Domestic Wire	27	24	24	24	-	-	25

A Variance report as shown above is designed to take the captured / aggregated volume of a line-item service and compare it to the previous month's volume. One could make an argument that the comparison should be to the average monthly volume for the service. Using an average monthly volume leads to the question of how many months should be used when developing an average? If you look too far back at history, you might find a point in time when a service was not being used at all. The most important thing is that the current (preliminary) volume is compared to something to help determine its' accuracy or validity.

The sample report design above compares the current preliminary volumes (Feb-25) for each service to the previous months (Jan-25) volumes. If a variance of more than 30% is found (higher or lower), then the percentage could be shown in another color such as RED, drawing attention to the line-item service for further review. The variance shown is intended to highlight what may be a problem. The variance does not mean there absolutely is a problem, but the higher the percentage in variance, the more likely that something could be wrong and needs further research.

This variance view is one of the very first reports one would use in operations to determine if the data collection process is complete and/or accurate. Other variance views will be used in the monthly analysis process, but this view is designed to make sure the volume side of the analysis equation (V*P) is accurate. Knowing there is no volume variance to be concerned about, service charge amount differences that may show up later in the monthly operational process, would likely point one to pricing issues.

Product and Service Variances Within Portfolio

Once satisfied that the volume differences for the entire bank are reasonable, another best practice during preliminary analysis verification is looking at variances that may exist amongst bank customers. The sample variance view below is designed to look at volume / activity differences for each of the customers in the bank. The best report design would support multiple data points including calculated service charge amounts. In this sample, the comparison is for total volumes from all services for each account. The current month's total volume is being compared to the average volume over the previous 12 months, looking for suspicious variances.

Product and Service Variances Within Portfolio - April 2025							
				>20% Variance-Service Volume		Difference Between Periods	
Account	Name	Officer Code	Opened Date	Last 12 Months Average Previous Period	Current Month Analysis Period	Difference	% Difference
1000	Hill Investments	21	8/22/2016	457	600	143	23.8%
5152	Johnson Industries		3/10/2014	35,685	60,664	24,979	41.2%
6045	Smith Consulting	10	1/1/2008	89,211	160,580	71,369	44.4%
10171	ABC Insurance		12/3/2015	39,010	12,690	(26,320)	-207.4%
10296	Alpha Corp	21	8/22/2016	26,879	6,498	(20,381)	-313.7%
10357	PSG Oil and Gas		8/24/2016	15,098	24,157	9,059	37.5%
10446	Goulds Bakery		1/22/2017	20,491	40,981	20,491	50.0%
12351	Davis Axles	4	7/25/2019	8,790	21,975	13,185	60.0%
13458	Bell Towers Ind	115	1/11/2008	142,738	385,393	242,655	63.0%
14985	Plymouth Rifles Inc		10/26/2017	23,795	38,072	14,277	37.5%
15092	Wonder White Bread		9/9/2009	6,587	11,198	4,611	41.2%
16789	Blueberry Company	1	1/1/2008	189,054	304,346	115,292	37.9%
16803	Allen Airways	1	3/19/2008	75,685	90,876	15,192	16.7%
17834	Cruise Two Travel	1	9/16/2009	53,527	78,907	25,380	32.2%
17901	Melvin Marketing	3	2/1/2015	3,984	6,374	2,390	37.5%
18567	Kool Carts Raceway	4	3/17/2008	35,685	71,369	35,685	50.0%
18932	Tiffany's Catering	115	12/19/2012	53,527	133,817	80,290	60.0%
19906	Office Supply Corp	59	12/1/2007	38,435	103,775	65,340	63.0%
19978	Kates Designs		3/31/2014	6,362	10,179	3,817	37.5%

Designed properly, a user should be able to produce a report like this using other averages in the compare process. Perhaps one would only be concerned with current volumes as compared to the previous month's volumes, or the average volume over the previous 3 months vs. the previous 12 months. More importantly, a user should be able to choose the data point for which they are searching for variance. A difference in total calculated charges for a customer could then be compared to charges of previous periods whether using an actual period or an average over many periods.

An operations person would seek out such variances in search of possible operational problems. The variance views could though, be of great interest to customer relationship / sales officers as well because if a customer had a high variance (and not due to an operational problem), there is a good chance something is going on with the customer and a conversation with them might be in order.

All too often through the years, I have seen such variance reporting stem from a decline in customer volumes resulting in lower customer fees, with the underlying issue being that the customer is leaving the bank.

Balance Variance Within Portfolio – Current Month

Variance reporting goes beyond products and services in account analysis. The balances associated with account analysis are also pertinent data points when searching for variance. The sample report below shows variance in the Average Net Ledger Balance.

Balance Variance Within Portfolio - April 2025

				Average Net Ledger		Difference Between Periods	
Account	Name	Officer Code	Opened Date	Previous Period	Analysis Period	Difference	% Difference
1000	Hill Investments	21	8/22/2016	$ 457	$ 600	$ 143	23.8%
5152	Johnson Industries		3/10/2014	$ 35,685	$ 60,664	$ 24,979	41.2%
6045	Smith Consulting	10	1/1/2008	$ 89,211	$ 160,580	$ 71,369	44.4%
10171	ABC Insurance		12/3/2015	$ 39,010	$ (58,514)	$ (97,524)	166.7%
10296	Alpha Corp	21	8/22/2016	$ 26,879	$ (61,822)	$ (88,701)	143.5%
10357	PSG Oil and Gas		8/24/2016	$ 15,098	$ 24,157	$ 9,059	37.5%
10446	Goulds Bakery		1/22/2017	$ 20,491	$ 40,981	$ 20,491	50.0%
12351	Davis Axles	4	7/25/2019	$ 8,790	$ 21,975	$ 13,185	60.0%
13458	Bell Towers Ind	115	1/11/2008	$ 142,738	$ 385,393	$ 242,655	63.0%
14985	Plymouth Rifles Inc		10/26/2017	$ 23,795	$ 38,072	$ 14,277	37.5%
15092	Wonder White Brea		9/9/2009	$ 6,587	$ 11,198	$ 4,611	41.2%
16789	Blueberry Company	1	1/1/2008	$ 113,527	$ 204,348	$ 90,821	44.4%
16803	Allen Airways	1	3/19/2008	$ 75,685	$ (113,527)	$ (189,211)	166.7%
17834	Cruise Two Travel	1	9/16/2009	$ 53,527	$ (123,112)	$ (176,638)	143.5%
17901	Melvin Marketing	3	2/1/2015	$ 3,984	$ 6,374	$ 2,390	37.5%
18567	Kool Carts Raceway	4	3/17/2008	$ 35,685	$ 71,369	$ 35,685	50.0%
18932	Tiffany's Catering	115	12/19/2012	$ 53,527	$ 133,817	$ 80,290	60.0%
19906	Office Supply Corp	59	12/1/2007	$ 38,435	$ 103,775	$ 65,340	63.0%
19978	Kates Designs		3/31/2014	$ 6,362	$ 10,179	$ 3,817	37.5%

A variance report like this though, increases in value if it works for other key data points for customers, like the Average Net Collected Balance, Average Negative Collected Balance, Earnings Allowance, etc. A faulty earnings credit rate for example could easily throw off an account's earnings allowance. A fee disposition error could quickly turn compensable service charges into hard charges, causing havoc in the account analysis operations department.

In designing a report such as shown above, building in the capability of running the report for other data points would be the best practice and create a more powerful tool. The search for variance is often situational so designing a report like this should support the flexibility of selecting from a list of pertinent data points.

Debit, Credit, and Invoice Register – Current Month

This report example is often referred to as a Debit Register because most accounts shown on this report will likely only have an auto-debit amount displayed. The totals shown for any given month would likely correlate to the same report from previous months. Any drastic differences in the totals should be explainable by those involved. Did the bank acquire another bank and therefore the number of accounts has greatly increased? Did the default earnings allowance rate(s) rise therefore making it possible for the same / similar customer balances involved to cover more of the analysed fees?

Debit, Credit, and Invoice Register by Account - March 2025 *(Preliminary)*

							Invoice (Billing) Information			
Account Number	***Name***	***Branch***	***Cost Center***	***Treasury Officer***	***Earned Credit***	***Fees Auto Debited***	***Fees Invoiced***	***Payments Past Due***	***Payments This Period***	***Interest Paid***
11111	ABC Industries	1003	1003	Bill Smith	$ 15.00	$ 156.78				
22222	DEF Global	2501	2501	Dave Robinson	$ 198.67	$ -				97.56
33333	GHI Corp	2502	2502	Helen Williams	$ 3.30	$ 768.09				
44444	Acme Industries	2001	2001	Judy Savage	$ 45.00	$ 503.29				
55555	Alpha Corp	2201	2201	Diane Price	$ 30.00	$ 493.39				
66666	Beta Corp	2501	2501	Tim Davis	$ 567.92	$ -				387.02
77777	Smith and Jones Inc	1502	1502	Kim Roberts	$ 12.96	$ 637.65				
88888	Davis Enterprises	3201	3201	Jane Simons	$ 12.00	$ -	$ 39.21	$ -	$ -	
99999	XYZ Corporation	2501	2501	Carie Smith	$ 40.00	$ 938.19				
111110	ABC Global Brands	2502	2502	Mark Davidson	$ 1.50	$ 916.67				
122221	Tech Track Corp	3501	3501	Bill Smith	$ 120.00	$ 120.00				
133332	Amber Insure	2501	2501	Carie Smith	$ 25.00	$ -	$ 167.89	$ 298.65	$ -	
144443	Southern Oil Corp	2501	2501	Dave Robinson	$ 100.00	$ 100.00				
155554	Northern Gas Corp	2501	2501	Diane Price	$ 25.00	$ 209.76				
166665	Blue Sky Dental	2501	2501	Helen Williams	$ 23.00	$ 782.09				
177776	Nelson Medical	2506	2506	Jane Simons	$ 1.50	$ 125.62				
188887	Davis Industries	3500	3500	Judy Savage	$ 50.00	$ 732.56				
199998	Global Brands	8001	8001	Kim Roberts	$ 75.00	$ 24.89				
211109	International Coal	8002	8002	Tim Davis	$ 12.00	$ 11,569.98				
					$ 1,357.85	**$ 18,078.96**	**$ 207.10**	**$ 298.65**	**$ -**	**$ 484.58**

Because a bank will likely have some accounts that are invoiced for their treasury management fees, the report captures invoice information as well. If any interest was paid to an account, that too is captured here. Basically, anything affecting the bank's general ledger accounts as they relate to fee income, interest expense, or accounts receivable are captured on this report. Best practices support the creation of a report like this whether it is the result of a preliminary or final analysis. The reason for this is that the preliminary creation of this report can then be used to detect any problems with the month's analysis before it becomes final.

An operational report like this also serves as an audit trail for the account analysis department. When this report is generated after final analysis, it then represents all debits and credits generated by the analysis system and passed on to the demand deposit / general ledger systems. The customer's statement would have to be used to determine what details lie beneath a particular debit / credit amount.

Service Volume Usage Analysis by Service Disposition

One often overlooked data view in analysis operations is a Service Volume Usage Analysis report. This report allows one to see all the activity-based services and the volumes involved at each distinct unit price. The data source for such a report is all line-item services that appear on analysis statements. The operations department will have specific expectations of volumes used by services and the unit prices involved so a data-view like this is extremely helpful in confirming expectations (or creating cause for concern). This report shows a very high-level view of services based on the entirety of the bank's analysis statements.

Service Volume Usage Analysis by Service Disposition - April 2025

Service Code	Description	Unit Price	Volume	Charge	Expense	Marginal Profit	Fee Disposition
1001	Monthly Maintenance	$ 10.00	2	$ 20.00	$ 17.00	$ 3.00	A-Analyzed
1001	Monthly Maintenance	$ 15.00	21	$ 315.00	$ 267.75	$ 47.25	A-Analyzed
1001	Monthly Maintenance	$ 20.00	11	$ 220.00	$ 187.00	$ 33.00	A-Analyzed
1001	Monthly Maintenance	$ 25.00	344	$ 8,600.00	$ 7,310.00	$ 1,290.00	A-Analyzed
1004	Deposits	$ 0.75	50	$ 37.50	$ 31.88	$ 5.63	A-Analyzed
1004	Deposits	$ 0.40	5	$ 2.00	$ 1.70	$ 0.30	A-Analyzed
1004	Deposits	$ 0.25	40	$ 10.00	$ 8.50	$ 1.50	A-Analyzed
1005	Items Deposited	$ 0.15	400	$ 60.00	$ 51.00	$ 9.00	A-Analyzed
1005	Items Deposited	$ 0.15	55	$ 8.25	$ 7.01	$ 1.24	F-Fee Based
1005	Items Deposited	$ 0.12	32	$ 3.84	$ 3.26	$ 0.58	A-Analyzed

The data view above highlights that a service may be priced uniquely within the bank's portfolio of accounts. This data view often creates cause for concern and requires further research, which is the reason a report like this is actionable. A bank's operations team knows the pricing for their services rather well and might be alarmed to see that 55 items of the service known as *Items Deposited* are F-Fee Based (non-compensable).

An operations team will also be alarmed to find a unit price being used somewhere when it wasn't expected. For example, the operations team might assume that all deposits are priced at $0.75 each, so seeing anything except $0.75 being used would be cause for concern and require further research as to why.

The concerns described above demonstrate the need for powerful search capabilities within an analysis system. One simplistic approach would be to search an entire text file of statements for the text string "*Deposits $ 0.25*". This search would bring one directly to the account number using such. A more refined approach would be a search tool built right into the system where one could enter search criteria focused on Service Code, Volume, Unit Price, etc. The result of such a search should show which account numbers / names have such pricing, taking operational users directly to the source of concern.

Product Management Reporting

Overview

The sample reports and data views following are entirely focused on treasury management product categories. The data views were designed for anyone involved with product management. Product categories are closely aligned to different departments within a bank, so these data views are of great interest to the ACH Origination department or the Wire Room for example.

The data views shown in this section present a design methodology I refer to as *drill through* reporting. The designs basically present information in what I will call a *collapsed* view but then allow for one to drill into specific information to review more detail by expanding (drilling into) the summary data. This technique is very fitting for treasury management due to the nature of product categories and the service line items that make up each category. Even when looking at line-item services, there is more granular detail to be seen when you consider the price and fee disposition of a single line-item service.

Service Fee Disposition

Given all the service line-items found within a specific product category, most will typically be *analyzed* services. These analyzed services are also known as compensable services because an account's earnings allowance can offset (or compensate for) these service charges. Some services will possibly have a *fee-based* disposition, meaning they are being charged in full regardless of any earnings allowance. Some analysis systems refer to fee-based services as hard charged services (even *explicit charge* services). Still others support both *fee-based* and *hard-charged* services with the difference being the frequency as to when they are taken from an account.

Line-item services that are set to *waive* will show a calculated service charge, but there really is no revenue gained. Some analysis systems support a service disposition that equates to a service fee that was debited in another system previously (like the demand deposit system). This disposition became important for any bank that wanted to see all fees debited to an account on one single statement regardless of the service fee being calculated by the account analysis system or debited in some other system. This practice of showing already debited service charges is not considered to be the best practice, as it can be confusing to customers (a customer would think they are getting charged twice).

For purposes of suggested report designs following, I refer to service fee dispositions as A-Analyzed, F-Fee Based, W-Waived, and D-Directly Debited. If for some reason your analysis data has additional fee disposition categories, you would certainly include them as a part of your own reporting plan / design.

Revenue by Product Category

My first reporting example is intended to display account analysis results in a *Summary of all Revenue by Product Category* for a specific Month and Year. This summary is focused on the accumulated Revenue from each Product Category along with the actual accumulated volumes from service activity within the category. By taking an aggregated revenue figure and dividing it by an aggregated volume figure, one can determine the average unit price for an entire Product Category across all the line-item services within. This summary aggregates all service data for the Product Category regardless of whether a service fee is analyzed, waived, hard charged, fee based, or directly debited in an external system.

Revenue by Product Category - March 2025

Product Category	Description	Volume	Average Unit Price	Revenue	Average Unit Cost	Expense	Profit	Margin %	Product Categroy Sequence
+ DEP	Depository Services	20	0.7500	$ 15.00	$ 0.6000	$ 12.00	$ 3.00	20.0%	1
+ RDC	Remote Deposit Capture	54	0.2400	$ 12.96	$ 0.1920	$ 10.37	$ 2.59	20.0%	2
+ ACH	**ACH Origination**	44	3.4784	$ 153.05	$ 2.7555	$ 121.24	$ 31.81	20.8%	3
+ OLB	Online Banking	1	12.0000	$ 12.00	$ 9.6000	$ 9.60	$ 2.40	20.0%	4
+ POS	Positive Pay	1	45.0000	$ 45.00	$ 36.0000	$ 36.00	$ 9.00	20.0%	5
+ RPP	Reverse Positive Pay	1	30.0000	$ 30.00	$ 24.0000	$ 24.00	$ 6.00	20.0%	6
+ WIR	Wire Transfer	13	13.0769	$ 170.00	$ 10.4615	$ 136.00	$ 34.00	20.0%	7
+ SWP	Funds Management	1	25.0000	$ 25.00	$ 20.0000	$ 20.00	$ 5.00	20.0%	8
+ IFT	Integrated Funds Transf	1	100.0000	$ 100.00	$ 80.0000	$ 80.00	$ 20.00	20.0%	9
+ LBX	Lockbox	121	0.7190	$ 87.00	$ 0.5752	$ 69.60	$ 17.40	20.0%	10
		257	**2.5292**	**$ 650.01**	**$ 2.0187**	**$ 518.81**	**$ 131.20**	**20.2%**	

In this example, there is an acronym assigned to each product category. A code like this is commonly used in various displays in the event the full Product Category description is not used. A product becomes very identifiable by users simply by using intuitive acronyms like LBX for Lockbox.

The Volume shown is basically the aggregated value of all services and their volumes within each Product Category. Given the total Revenue, the report can develop an average unit price. In account analysis, the Total Expense for a volume-based service is the volume times the unit cost. If one were to aggregate all the expenses for a product category, an average unit cost is easily calculated by diving the Total Expense by the Total Volume.

The difference between revenue and expense for services could be categorized as gross profit or gross margin. In this example above, it appears as if the unit cost on all services has been set to 80% of the unit price for all services, thus yielding a 20% margin across the board. I've included a product category sequence number here because management may prefer a specific reporting sequence when it comes to numerous treasury management products.

Note these product categories are much like product categories seen in the AFP coding of products and services. One could consider adding the AFP product code to the display (ACH Origination for example, is AFP Product Code 25). The codes for each AFP product category have been intentionally left out to keep the display clear and concise.

I often refer to the report display shown previously as a spreadsheet view (rows and columns of numbers). While the detail of any such view is important, some people are more visual and prefer a visualisation of the data.

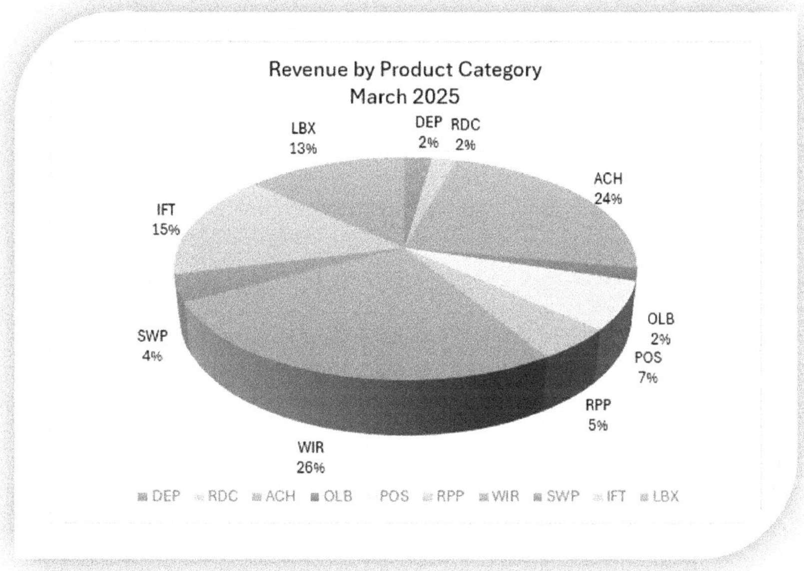

A graphical depiction of the same data is shown above. This visual instantly shows the viewer that the bank's wire revenue is more significant than any other treasury management product in the bank. Note the use of product category acronyms here, sometimes there simply isn't the space to show complete product descriptions. Like the spreadsheet view of this same data, the data view represents a single month of revenue for the bank.

The next report sample is very similar to this one except that it drills into just a bit more detail surrounding the revenue of a specific product category.

Product Category Revenue by Disposition

This summary is focused on the accumulated Revenue from each Product Category along with the actual accumulated volumes from service activity within the Product Category. The Product Revenue shown here is *drilled into* though, based upon the service dispositions found within each Product Category. The Product Revenue is more detailed in nature as it is displayed based upon the service Disposition (Analyzed, Fee Based, Waived, and Direct Debit).

Product Category Revenue by Disposition - March 2025

Product Category	Description	Disposition	Volume	Unit Price	Revenue	Unit Cost	Expense	Profit	Margin%
+ DEP	Depository Services	A-Analyzed	20	0.7500	$ 15.00	$ 0.6000	$ 12.00	$ 3.00	20.0%
+ RDC	Remote Deposit Capture	A-Analyzed	54	0.2400	$ 12.96	$ 0.1920	$ 10.37	$ 2.59	20.0%
+ ACH	ACH Origination	A-Analyzed	32	3.1266	$ 100.05	$ 2.5013	$ 80.04	$ 20.01	20.0%
+ ACH	ACH Origination	F-Fee Based	1	25.0000	$ 25.00	$ 20.0000	$ 20.00	$ 5.00	20.0%
+ ACH	ACH Origination	W-Waived	11	2.5455	$ 28.00	$ 1.9273	$ 21.20	$ 6.80	24.3%
+ OLB	Online Banking	A-Analyzed	1	12.0000	$ 12.00	$ 9.6000	$ 9.60	$ 2.40	20.0%
+ POS	Positive Pay	A-Analyzed	1	45.0000	$ 45.00	$ 36.0000	$ 36.00	$ 9.00	20.0%
+ RPP	Reverse Positive Pay	A-Analyzed	1	30.0000	$ 30.00	$ 24.0000	$ 24.00	$ 6.00	20.0%
+ WIR	Wire Transfer	A-Analyzed	13	13.0769	$ 170.00	$ 10.4615	$ 136.00	$ 34.00	20.0%
+ SWP	Funds Management	A-Analyzed	1	25.0000	$ 25.00	$ 20.0000	$ 20.00	$ 5.00	20.0%
+ IFT	Integrated Funds Transfer	F-Fee Based	1	100.0000	$ 100.00	$ 80.0000	$ 80.00	$ 20.00	20.0%
+ LBX	Lockbox	A-Analyzed	120	0.1000	$ 12.00	$ 0.0800	$ 9.60	$ 2.40	20.0%
+ LBX	Lockbox	W-Waived	-	0.0000	$ -	$ -	$ -	$ -	0.0%
+ LBX	Lockbox	F-Fee Based	1	75.0000	$ 75.00	$ 60.0000	$ 60.00	$ 15.00	20.0%
			257	**2.5292**	**$ 650.01**	**$ 2.0187**	**$ 518.81**	**$ 131.20**	**20.2%**

While the example display above is very similar to the Revenue by Product Category example, you can tell there is a more detailed breakdown of the calculated revenue in the system by looking at *ACH Origination*. The revenue associated with *ACH Origination* has varying fee dispositions because 32 of the items were calculated as A-Analyzed services, 1 of the ACH-Originated items was considered F-Fee Based, and the final 11 items were all calculated and waived (not actually charged to the customer).

If I were the product manager for *ACH Origination*, the fee- based and/or the waived service fees shown may (or may not) be cause for concern. This more detailed view of the bank's revenue highlights the importance of *fee disposition* in account analysis. A graphical depiction of fee disposition for a single product family (ACH Origination) is shown below:

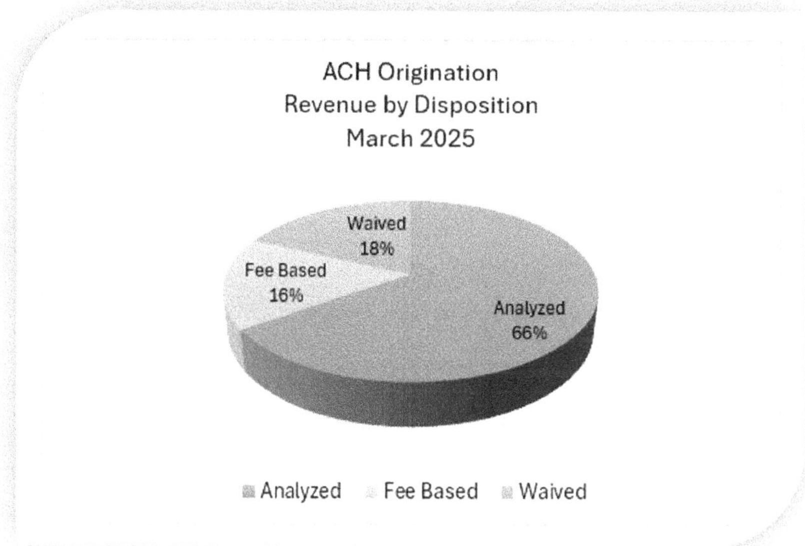

Product Category Revenue by Service

The example design for this report is intended to display account analysis results for each individual service line-item within each Product Category. The display below only includes ACH Origination services but given the service data is organized within each Product Category the sample below could have included all services for all categories.

Product Category Revenue by Service - March 2025

	Product Category	Bank Service ID Code	Description	Accounts Using	Volume	Average Unit Price	Revenue	Average Unit Cost	Expense	Profit	Margin%
+	**ACH**	**2501**	**ACH Maintenance**	4	4	$ 35.00	$ 140.00	$28.0000	$ 112.00	$ 28.00	20.0%
+	ACH	2502	ACH Debits	2	32	$ 0.15	$ 4.80	$ 0.1200	$ 3.84	$ 0.96	20.0%
+	ACH	2503	ACH Credits	1	5	$ 0.15	$ 0.75	$ 0.1200	$ 0.60	$ 0.15	20.0%
+	ACH	2504	ACH Returned Items	-	-	$ -	$ -	$ -	$ -	$ -	0.0%
+	ACH	2505	ACH Files Originated	-	-	$ -	$ -	$ -	$ -	$ -	0.0%
+	ACH	2506	ACH NOCs	1	3	$ 2.00	$ 6.00	$ 1.6000	$ 4.80	$ 1.20	20.0%
					44	**$ 3.44**	**152**	**$ 2.7555**	**121**	**$ 30.31**	**20.0%**

The first new data element you see above is the Bank Service ID Code. The AFP references this code as the BIC-Bank Identifying Code. In all these cases, it simply refers to a code that is used to identify a service within the bank. It is a bank assigned code, and people within the bank would be able to identify a service with this code. Like the Product Category code / acronym, the bank service code is often used in addition to or in place of the complete service description. Here above, both the code and the description are shown because the report view design allows the real estate to show both.

You will notice another new column in the design above called *Accounts Using*. This report design element turns this report into a usage analysis report. This report shows that two different accounts have used the service known as *ACH Debits*. There was a total of 32 *ACH Debits* used but only two accounts had used them. All the other columns of the report design are the same as previous samples in terms of total revenue, expense, and margin. In this design though, the breakdown is about the individual line- item services within a given Product Category.

Some data warehouse systems would allow custom report designs, driven by known data. In the sample below, a chart is created for Revenue by Product / Service Code. The design is such that a user could select the Product Category and timeframe, to plot any of a variety of data points, in this sample it is Gross Revenue.

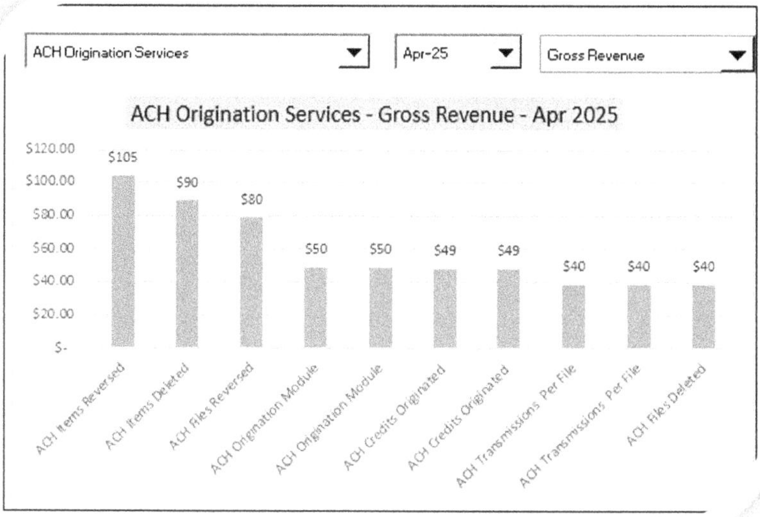

Service Code Revenue by Unit Price

When viewing a display that includes the detail line-item services (each Service Code) one could possibly drill into that data for a couple of reasons. As shown previously, one reason might be to see the fee disposition (and usage) of each service code (Analyzed, Waived, etc.). Another reason one may want to drill into the detail of a specific service code would be to see the distinct unit prices being used across the bank for the service code in question.

Service Code Revenue by Unit Price - April 2025

	Product Category	Bank Service ID Code	Description	Accounts Using	Volume	Unit Price	Revenue	Disposition	Average Unit Cost	Expense	Profit	Margin%
+	**ACH**	**2501**	**ACH Maintenance**	2	2	$ 25.00	$ 50.00	A-Analyzed	$ 20.0000	$ 40.00	$ 10.00	20.0%
+	ACH	2501	ACH Maintenance	1	1	$ 40.00	$ 40.00	A-Analyzed	$ 32.0000	$ 32.00	$ 8.00	20.0%
+	ACH	2501	ACH Maintenance	1	1	$ 50.00	$ 50.00	A-Analyzed	$ 40.0000	$ 40.00	$ 10.00	20.0%

Shown above is the result of drilling into the ACH Maintenance Service Code. This display reveals that four (4) accounts are using the ACH Maintenance service. The collapsed display shown previously indicates the revenue from this ACH Maintenance service is a total of $140 but this more granular version of the display shows that two (2) accounts used a unit price of $25, another account used a unit price of $40, and the last account involved used a unit price of $50.

Having this information at the fingertips of revenue management staff is important because some of this pricing shown may be due to an error of some sort and require further investigation.

Service Code Unit Price Usage by Account

The beauty of this design is that now the distinct unit price lines for this service code can be selected for even further evaluation. *Drilling into* a specific unit price for a specific service code now allows one to see the detail account numbers that are using each of the distinct prices above. The two accounts using a unit price of $25 for ACH Maintenance are shown here.

Service Code Unit Price Usage by Account - April 2025

Account Number	Name	Product Category	Bank Service ID Code	Description	Volume	Unit Price	Revenue	Disposition	Average Unit Cost	Expense	Profit	Margin%
11111	ABC Industries	ACH	2501	ACH Maintenance	1	$ 25.00	$ 25.00	A-Analyzed	$20.0000	$ 20.00	$ 5.00	20.0%
44444	123 Services, Inc	ACH	2501	ACH Maintenance	1	$ 25.00	$ 25.00	A-Analyzed	$20.0000	$ 20.00	$ 5.00	20.0%

Service Code Revenue by Account

As mentioned above, one may want to drill into the details of a specific service code for specific reasons. The fee disposition of each service is one reason and the distinct unit prices being used for a service is certainly another. Perhaps a more common reason to drill into a specific service code is to simply see all the accounts using the service and the revenue associated with each account.

Service Code Revenue by Account - April 2025

Account Number	Name	Product Category	Bank Service ID Code	Description	Price Source	Volume	Unit Price	Revenue	Disposition	Average Unit Cost	Expense	Profit	Margin%
11111	ABC Industries	ACH	2501	ACH Maintenance	12328	1	$ 25.00	$ 25.00		$20.0000	$ 20.00	$ 5.00	20.0%
22222	DEF Insurance	ACH	2501	ACH Maintenance	99999	1	$ 50.00	$ 50.00		$40.0000	$ 40.00	$ 10.00	20.0%
33333	XYZ Corporation	ACH	2501	ACH Maintenance	32128	1	$ 40.00	$ 40.00		$32.0000	$ 32.00	$ 8.00	20.0%
44444	123 Services, Inc	ACH	2501	ACH Maintenance	12328	1	$ 25.00	$ 25.00		$20.0000	$ 20.00	$ 5.00	20.0%

To this point, the product reporting examples have been based upon the current month. All the content shown represents a single month of treasury management activity. The samples that follow dive into trend reporting, meaning that we will see a similar view of the same data but in this case, over time.

P x V Revenue by Product Group – Last 13 Months

The term **P x V** is often used in describing treasury services. This reference is to the calculation of volume multiplied by the unit price for each individual service. The calculation describes a gross view of revenue (before any earnings credit). The data view below illustrates how one would do a **P x V** display of all the services within each product group.

P x V Revenue Trend by Product Group - March 2025

Product Group	Description	2024 Mar	2024 Apr	2024 May	2024 Jun	2024 Jul	2024 Aug	2024 Sep	2024 Oct	2024 Nov	2024 Dec	2025 Jan	2025 Feb	2025 Mar	2025 YTD
+ DEP	Depository Services	$ 13.50	$ 13.65	$ 13.80	$ 13.95	$ 14.10	$ 15.30	$ 14.25	$ 15.45	$ 14.40	$ 15.15	$ 14.70	$ 15.15	$ 15.00	$ 44.85
+ RDC	Remote Deposit Capture	$ 11.66	$ 11.79	$ 11.92	$ 12.05	$ 12.18	$ 13.22	$ 12.31	$ 13.35	$ 12.44	$ 13.09	$ 12.70	$ 13.09	$ 12.96	$ 38.75
+ ACH	**ACH Origination**	$ 137.75	$ 139.28	$ 140.81	$ 142.34	$ 143.87	$ 156.11	$ 145.40	$ 157.64	$ 146.93	$ 154.58	$ 149.99	$ 154.58	$ 153.05	$ 457.62
+ OLB	Online Banking	[illegible]	[illegible]	[illegible]	[illegible]	[illegible]	[illegible]	$ 11.10	[illegible]	[illegible]	$ 12.10	[illegible]	[illegible]	[illegible]	[illegible]
+ POS	Positive Pay	$ 40.50	$ 40.95	$ 41.40	$ 41.85	$ 42.30	$ 45.90	$ 42.75	$ 46.35	$ 43.20	$ 45.45	$ 44.10	$ 45.45	$ 45.00	$ 134.55
+ RPP	Reverse Positive Pay	$ 27.00	$ 27.30	$ 27.60	$ 27.90	$ 28.20	$ 30.60	$ 28.50	$ 30.90	$ 28.80	$ 30.30	$ 29.40	$ 30.30	$ 30.00	$ 89.70
+ WIR	Wire Transfer	$ 153.00	$ 154.70	$ 156.40	$ 158.10	$ 159.80	$ 173.40	$ 161.50	$ 175.10	$ 163.20	$ 171.70	$ 166.60	$ 171.70	$ 170.00	$ 508.30
+ SWP	Funds Management	$ 22.50	$ 22.75	$ 23.00	$ 23.25	$ 23.50	$ 25.50	$ 23.75	$ 25.75	$ 24.00	$ 25.25	$ 24.50	$ 25.25	$ 25.00	$ 74.75
+ IFT	Integrated Funds Transfer	$ 90.00	$ 91.00	$ 92.00	$ 93.00	$ 94.00	$ 102.00	$ 95.00	$ 103.00	$ 96.00	$ 101.00	$ 98.00	$ 101.00	$ 100.00	$ 299.00
+ LBX	Lockbox	$ 78.30	$ 79.17	$ 80.04	$ 80.91	$ 81.78	$ 88.74	$ 82.65	$ 89.61	$ 83.52	$ 87.87	$ 85.26	$ 87.87	$ 87.00	$ 260.13
		$ 585.01	**$ 591.51**	**$ 598.01**	**$ 604.51**	**$ 611.01**	**$ 663.01**	**$ 617.51**	**$ 669.51**	**$ 624.01**	**$ 656.51**	**$ 637.01**	**$ 656.51**	**$ 650.01**	**$ 1,943.53**

The same data can be represented graphically using an area chart as shown here.

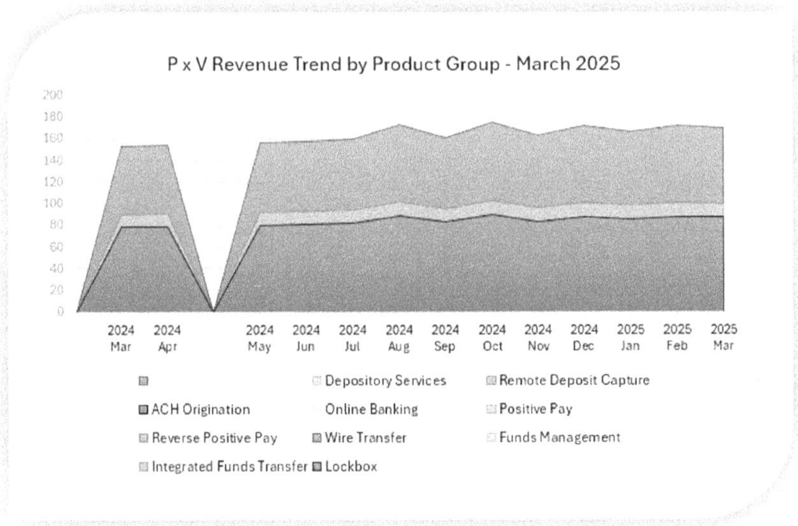

Sales Management Reporting

Overview

With Sales Management Reporting in account analysis, the focus changes from product / service codes and categories to treasury management sales officers and how productive each one is based upon the account analysis data. The sample views below focus on new relationships / accounts but just as important, new products sold to existing accounts as well. The views place importance on the revenue created from all the activity on assigned accounts by officer, but also on ROL-Revenue Opportunity Lost by officer. Said another way, ROL represents concessions, discounts, and waivers. Generating $1,000 in revenue from a customer each month has little meaning if it is all being waived. In this context, concession pricing, discounts, and waivers are viewed as the responsibility of each treasury officer assigned to accounts that have such concessions. Candidly, a treasury management salesperson at *Your National Bank* could sell a lot of services if the price was free.

Officer Review Summary

The Officer Review Summary is designed to show sales management a high-level view of each treasury sales officer and the accounts they manage. The totals could be for a team, a market, a sales manager, etc. and will vary based upon how the bank's sales staff is organized. The important data elements here are how many accounts each officer is managing as well as the fee income (and ROL) associated with each treasury officer. The effective earnings allowance rate is found by dividing the earnings allowance totals by the total net average collected balance. A data view like this is an actionable view. I'd like to ask John Lynch why he has the most accounts of anyone yet the lowest amount of fee income?

Officer Review Summary - March 2025

Officer Code	Officer Name	Chargeable Accounts	Average Net Ledger Balance	Average Net Collected Balance	Effective Earnings Credit Rate	Earnings Allowance	Analyzed Charges Before Credit	Total Fees Debited	Revenue Opportunity Lost	Interest Paid
+ BEH	Beth Hossner	8	$ 2,435,189	$ 2,290,969	0.31%	$ 597	$ 1,675	$ 1,078	$ 223	$ -
+ JPB	Joseph Banks	6	$ 777,420	$ 741,925	0.28%	$ 175	$ 854	$ 679	$ 29	$ -
+ REB	Robert Bean	6	$ 343,364	$ 311,077	0.01%	$ 3	$ 403	$ 400	$ 15	$ -
+ JDL	John D Lynch	16	$ 368,765	$ 340,398	0.00%	$ -	$ 93	$ 93	$ 20	$ -
	Team Johnson	**36**	**$ 3,924,738**	**$ 3,684,369**	**0.25%**	**$ 775**	**$ 3,025**	**$ 2,250**	**$ 287**	**$ -**

The information in the data view shown above is taken directly from the account analysis statement for the accounts in question. The next data view drills into more detailed information for new products sold to the account base. A graphical depiction of the total fee income for each treasury officer is shown below:

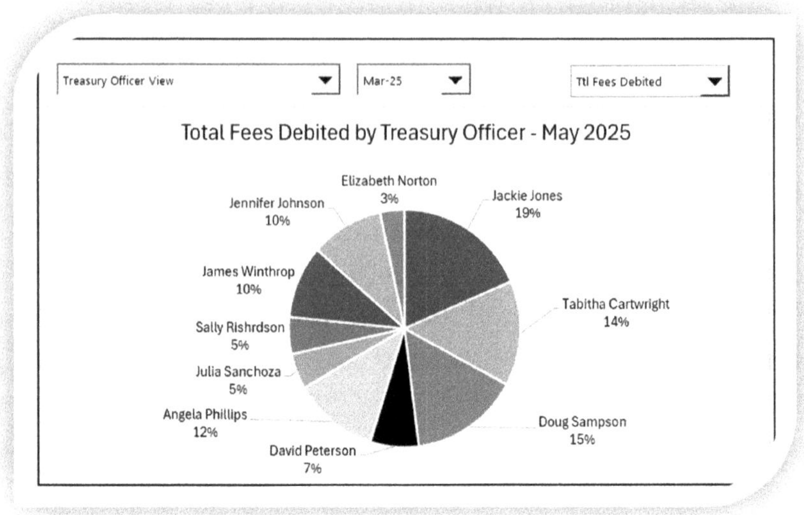

New Products by Account for each Treasury Officer – Current Month

The New Products by Account report is indicative of the successful sales activity for each officer. The focus is on new treasury management products vs. new customers.

New Products by Account for each Treasury Officer - April 2025													
Officer Code	*Officer Name*	*Account Number*	*Customer Name*	*DEP*	*RDC*	*ACH*	*OLB*	*POS*	*RPP*	*WIR*	*SWP*	*IFT*	*LBX*
+ BEH	Beth Hossner	50061232	Peaceful Valley Farm Supply			1							
+ BEH	Beth Hossner	1465009	Cascade Electrical							1	1		
+ REB	Robert Bean	2869007	Urban Renovation Services				1						
+ JDL	John D Lynch	4580346	Summit Trucking								1		
	Team Johnson			0		1	1	0	0	1	2	0	0

This view shows what new products customers have signed up for. The concept may lead one to wonder how one would create such a data view. In one implementation of this data view, I concluded that if a customer has a specific treasury product this month but did not have that same treasury product last month (and even the month before as well) the customer must have subscribed to the product this month. Since accounts are specifically assigned to treasury management salespeople, one could conclude that the salesperson assigned should get credit and/or take responsibility for the sale of that product. In essence, one can create the data view above simply by looking at account analysis statement history for the customer.

Because treasury management products most commonly have monthly recurring maintenance fees, one could zone in on the presence of a maintenance fee service for each treasury product being analysed. If the service is present this month but was not present in either of the previous two months, one could conclude that the product was sold to the customer and should be reported as such.

The data view sample above shows which officer is involved, the account/customer that acquired the product, and a column for each possible product that may have been sold / acquired. An officer with or without activity could be shown within such a data view. In the sample above, I chose not to include an officer if they have had no sales activity for new products. This view is something I refer to as an actionable report. If over the course of a month a sales officer has no activity shown in this report, the question becomes why?

Perhaps the only thing that tops the success of selling a new product to an existing customer is selling an entirely new customer on switching their commercial account to Your National Bank! The next view focuses on new accounts and customers.

New Accounts & Relationships by Treasury Officer

Like the New Products data view above, this data view is focused on the success of each treasury management sales officer. Instead of showing specific products however, this data view simply focuses on new accounts brought into the bank and the sales officer responsible for these accounts.

Just like the New Products report, this data view becomes actionable when a treasury office never shows up on this data view. This is a monthly report highlighting the activity that occurred within the previous month.

New Accounts & Relationships by Treasury Officer - March 2025

Officer Code	Officer Name	Account Number	Customer Name	Date Opened	Average Net Collected Balance	Effective Earnings Credit Rate	Earnings Allowance	Analyzed Charges Before Credit	Total Fees Debited	Revenue Opportunity Lost	Interest Paid
+ JEJ	James Jones	7354672	Justice IT Enterprises	3/12/2025	$ 1,365,879	0.24%	$ 275	$ 870	$ 595	$ 120	$ -
+ JEJ	James Jones	8651254	Andover Asphalt	3/15/2025	$ 325,097	0.34%	$ 92	$ 487	$ 395	$ 15	$ -
+ DTS	Dave Sebastian	9678436	Lindberger Restaurants	3/26/2025	$ 150,956	0.33%	$ 42	$ 225	$ 183	$ 10	$ -
+ MSP	Mark Patterson	9856412	Destinos Restaurant	3/28/2025	$ 125,980	0.30%	$ 32	$ 46	$ 14	$ 5	$ -
	Team Davidson				**$ 1,967,912**	**0.27%**	**$ 441**	**$ 1,628**	**$ 1,187**	**$ 150**	**$ -**

This view shows new customers and the date when they were opened. The report also shows the balances and the income immediately attributable to the new account / customer. Each new account is shown in this view, and the accounts are organized by officer code. When seeking information for display on a report like this, one could focus on the date opened for each account. If for any reason the date opened field is not viable for selection criteria, it is also possible to use the same technique described for new products above. In other words, if the account was not analysis over the previous two months but now is showing as being on account analysis, it should be looked at as a new account that has been sold.

P x V Gross Revenue by Treasury Salesperson – Last 12 Months

Similar to the **P x V** Revenue by Product Category, the term "P x V" is here is referring to taking each individual service, and calculating the unit price times the volume for the service. The calculation describes a gross view of revenue (before any earnings credit is applied). The data view below illustrates how one would do a **P x V** display of all the services assigned to each treasury salesperson (as defined by the account level treasury officer code).

P x V Gross Revenue by Treasury Salesperson - March 2025

Treasury Salesperson	#Accounts	Apr-24	May-24	Jun-24	Jul-24	Aug-24	Sep-24	Oct-24	Nov-24	Dec-24	Jan-25	Feb-25	Mar-25	Total	Average
Jackie Jones	11	80	76	98	45	65	89	90	120	112	156	147	110	1188	99
Tabitha Cartwright	8	88	84	108	50	72	98	99	132	123	172	162	85	1271	106
Doug Sampson	9	76	72	93	43	62	85	86	114	106	148	140	90	1114	93
David Peterson	4	78	74	95	44	63	86	87	116	109	151	143	40	1086	90
Angela Phillips	7	104	99	127	59	85	116	117	156	146	203	191	70	1471	123
Julia Sanchoza	2	112	106	137	63	91	125	126	168	157	218	206	29	1538	128
Sally Rishrdson	3	69	65	84	39	56	77	77	103	96	134	126	30	957	80
James Winthrop	5	36	34	44	20	29	40	41	54	50	70	66	159	644	54
Jennifer Johnson	6	108	103	132	61	88	120	122	162	151	211	198	260	1715	143
Elizabeth Norton	2	112	106	137	63	91	125	126	168	157	218	206	20	1529	127
*** Team Total**	57	862	819	1,056	485	701	959	970	1,294	1,207	1,682	1,585	893	12,514	1,043

The data view above shows the number of accounts assigned to each treasury officer as well as the aggregated P x V of the service calculations. This view is a great depiction of the revenue produced by aggregating accounts for each salesperson and it is indicative of the salesperson's success over time. The analysis here specifically covers gross revenue before earnings credit.

Total Fees Due by Treasury Officer – Last 12 Months

Just like the P x V Revenue by Treasury Officer above, this data view is focused on revenue too but instead of gross P x V, this report is driven by total fees due after earnings credits are applied. The total is taken directly from analysis statements, and it represents net income summarized by salesperson / office code.

Total Fees Due After Credit by Treasury Salesperson - March 2025

Treasury Salesperson	#Accounts	Apr-24	May-24	Jun-24	Jul-24	Aug-24	Sep-24	Oct-24	Nov-24	Dec-24	Jan-25	Feb-25	Mar-25	Total	Average
Jackie Jones	11	72	68	88	41	59	80	81	108	101	140	132	99	1069	89
Tabitha Cartwright	8	77	73	94	43	62	85	86	115	107	149	141	74	1106	92
Doug Sampson	9	69	66	85	39	56	77	78	104	97	135	127	82	1014	84
David Peterson	4	71	68	87	40	58	79	80	107	100	139	131	37	999	83
Angela Phillips	7	97	92	118	54	79	108	109	145	135	189	178	65	1368	114
Julia Sanchoza	2	96	92	118	54	78	107	108	144	135	188	177	25	1323	110
Sally Rishrdson	3	60	57	73	34	49	67	67	90	84	117	110	26	833	69
James Winthrop	5	32	30	39	18	26	35	36	48	44	62	58	52	479	40
Jennifer Johnson	6	78	74	95	44	63	87	87	117	109	152	143	43	1091	91
Elizabeth Norton	2	88	84	108	50	72	98	100	133	124	173	163	16	1208	101
*** Team Total**	57	740	703	906	416	601	823	832	1110	1036	1443	1360	519	10489	874

Executive Management Reporting

Overview

Executive Management Reporting in account analysis would normally leave some of the analysis details aside and focus on overall performance within the bank. While both revenue and the associated opportunity loss are important metrics for example, which individual sales officers are responsible for such is typically not the concern of senior level management. The same could be said for billing points within product categories. Executive management would most certainly be interested to know that *ACH Origination* is perhaps the most profitable product being offered at the bank, but there would be little concern for *which* billing points within the ACH Origination category are generating that profitability.

The metrics within any account analysis system do formulate many interesting facts which would be of interest to senior bank management. Best practice is to make all the key metrics easily accessible to executive management in the form of KPIs – Key Performance Indicators.

Key Performance Indicators

The numerous data views prescribed previously above illustrate the enormity of actionable data contained within any account analysis system. Whether operations, product management, or sales management, financial institution executives often don't have the time or patience to tread through such detailed information.

When it comes to management reporting, higher level executives need higher level metrics to understand overall performance in commercial billing. While KPIs represent summarized values for very different components of account analysis, KPIs have similar attributes. First there is the KPI data point, which is *Net Revenue* in this example below. Following the data point is the period for which the data point is shown (the Month of May 2024). What gives the KPI meaning is a comparison to the same data point from a different point in time (in this case, May of 2023).

This sample KPI clearly shows Revenue is down more than 30% since May of 2023. A KPI can be made even more meaningful by including in any such design, a control leading to more information (or more functionality) within an application. In this case, an ellipses button is used in the top right portion of the KPI. The ellipses button in a design such as this could be used to allow a user to change the time-period involved, or possibly to view / export the underlying data being used to create the summary KPI in the first place.

Every KPI reported from a commercial billing system should have a reliable data source showing the underlying detail involved with creating the KPI. In the case of Net Revenue, the sample report (shown above) called *Debit, Credit, and Invoice Register* would be the perfect underlying data source for the Net Revenue KPI because the report shows every account level fee taken via auto debit or billed via invoice for the month in question.

While the sample KPI shown above measures Net Revenue for a single month and the difference between two different points in time, a single month view of Net Revenue (or any other data point for that matter) may not tell the whole story. Many financial reporting systems use Year To Date (YTD) information but I have found this time-period to be of minimal use in the early portion of any fiscal year. I have always felt that looking at a sum (or average) over a time-period like the last 12 running months (L12M) to have more meaning than any YTD summarization.

The KPI shown above is showing the total Net Revenue for the last 12 running months through May 2024. A comparison is being made to the L12M for the same data point through May 2023 and a 10% difference is being reflected. Any programming behind the ellipses shown could show a variety of options including those previously mentioned plus now the ability to look at a *sum* over the time periods involved or an *average* over the time periods involved.

An average for any data point over the previous 12 running months can be very meaningful and even help one predict the monthly periods to come for budgeting purposes. Account analysis is a monthly system with a billing event that happens once per/month. Reporting of most data points is for an individual month making time metrics of Current Month, Last Month, Quarter to Date, Year to Date, and Last 12 Running months all very meaningful. KPIs in account analysis would have little meaning for any metric from day to day within a given month.

Through dates, time periods, comparisons to other time periods, and percentage differences will always be of interest when looking at a key performance indicator, leaving only the data points in question. Imagine the ability to see KPIs as described above for data points meaningful to account analysis such as:

- **$ Complete Account or Relationship Waivers**
- **$ Service Line-Item Waivers**
- **$ Revenue Opportunity Lost (Includes All Waivers)**
- **$ Interest Paid**
- **$ Profitability Margin**
- **# Closed Accounts by Type**
- **# New Deposit Accounts on Account Analysis by Type**
- **# New Customer Relationships with 2+ Deposit Accounts**
- **# Account Level Service Pricing Exceptions**
- **# New Treasury Management Products Sold by Type**

When looking at KPIs in account analysis, a financial institution will likely want to focus on commercial analyzed accounts and non-analyzed (e.g. small business) accounts separately. A few of the metrics listed above use the term *Type* to depict compensable and non-compensable accounts.

Profitability and Revenue Ranking

Looking beyond KPIs, senior management also has a keen interest in knowing who the most profitable customers are at the bank. If the account analysis system being used is tracking both revenue and margin by customer, best practice would be to display top customers ranked either by their margin (profit) or the total revenue generated by the customer.

The data view below shows the top 15 customers ranked by their profit margin amount. Because the actual revenue ranking would be slightly different, this sample display shows the ranking for a customer whether it by based upon revenue or profit margin.

Profitability Ranking Report - Top 15 Customers Based On Profit - April 2025

				Revenue		Profitability	
Account Number	Name	Branch	Cost Center	Total Revenue	Revenue Rank	Total Profit	Profit Rank
66666	Beta Corp	2501	2501	$ 3,180.35	1	$ 1,749.19	1
22222	DEF Global	2501	2501	$ 1,112.55	2	$ 1,001.30	2
144443	Southern Oil Corp	2501	2501	$ 560.00	4	$ 504.00	3
122221	Tech Track Corp	3501	3501	$ 672.00	3	$ 403.20	4
199998	Global Brands	8001	8001	$ 420.00	5	$ 210.00	5
11111	ABC Industries	1003	1003	$ 84.00	13	$ 67.20	6
188887	Davis Industries	3500	3500	$ 280.00	6	$ 56.00	7
155554	Northern Gas Corp	2501	2501	$ 140.00	11	$ 56.00	8
166665	Blue Sky Dental	2501	2501	$ 128.80	12	$ 51.52	9
55555	Alpha Corp	2201	2201	$ 168.00	9	$ 50.40	10
44444	Acme Industries	2001	2001	$ 252.00	7	$ 50.40	11
99999	XYZ Corporation	2501	2501	$ 224.00	8	$ 44.80	12
133332	Amber Insure	2501	2501	$ 140.00	10	$ 42.00	13
88888	Davis Enterprises	3201	3201	$ 67.20	15	$ 40.32	14
77777	Smith and Jones Inc	1502	1502	$ 72.58	14	$ 36.29	15
				$ 7,501.48		**$ 4,362.62**	

Any development towards a data view as shown above should also consider the customers who are the bottom dwellers. The 15 worst customers based on profit margin likely have numerous fee waivers. Such waivers ruin a customer's margin because while there is no revenue, there still is a cost.

PART III: Bank Fee Monitoring & Best Practices

In the corporate treasury world where account analysis statements are received, there is a propensity to verify the accuracy of such statements. There is a correlation though between the total amount of fees due on such statements and how much time / effort a business will allocate to a proper verification of those fees.

Imagine a small business where bank fees are $1k for the entire year vs. a multi-national corporation paying $2.5m in bank fees per/year. Through time, many bank fee monitoring software vendors have touted that they've found errors in bank fees totaling as much as 15% of total fees due. Given this information, imagine how much a business might be willing to spend in search of these errors. In the case of a small business paying $1k annually, the analysis statement(s) outlining these fees, are likely not even being looked at.

Time has proven that if a business is not paying at least $250k in bank fees per/year, the business cannot justify the costs involved with doing bank fee monitoring in a completely automated fashion using a licensed vendor solution. The chapters that follow describe where bank fee monitoring places focus, as well as the varying methodologies for doing the monitoring and verification of bank fees.

Twelve

Bank Fees - What Could Possibly Be Wrong?

Account Balances

When monitoring bank fees and doing bank fee analysis, one doesn't normally think that account balances have anything to do with it. The fact is, monitoring account balances is very much a part of bank fee monitoring, starting with the basic math of how balances are used in commercial account analysis.

Calculating an earnings credit allowance is a very important step in determining the total fees debited each month so all aspects of this calculation are typically covered by bank fee monitoring systems. Every balance in account analysis has an AFP Code associated with it. Bank fee monitoring systems will use this AFP Code to understand the balance being sent and then do internal calculations to ensure that the basic math is correct. For example, by definition the Average Net Collected Balance (AFP Code 00 00 10) must be equal to the Average Net Ledger Balance (AFP Code 00 00 00) less the Average Float Balance (AFP Code 00 00 30).

When it comes to applying the earnings credit rate (ECR) to the accounts Average Positive Collected Balance (AFP Code 00 00 11), monitoring software will also ensure the Earnings Allowance (AFP Code 00 02 40) is calculated properly.

These internal calculations are performed to help statement receivers understand exactly what they are getting from each of their banks. Imagine if a bank calculated the earnings allowance using the Average Net Collected Balance and then also assessed an uncollected funds fee for drawing into uncollected funds. This is commonly referred to as "double dipping" in analysis because the earnings allowance is being penalized for the draw into uncollected funds and a separate charge is also being assessed for the draw. A premium bank fee monitoring system would identify this situation and raise it as an issue.

Bank fee monitoring systems also look for balance fluctuations as months go by. Large fluctuations can be cause for concern. At the very least, large balance reductions are an early warning that an account is / may no longer being used by the organization.

Line-Item Services

The AFP Service Codes were originally designed to describe and explicitly define all the bank services seen on account analysis statements. The thought was that if a bank would attach an AFP Service Code to each of their services where fees are being generated, then any receiver of an account analysis statement could make better sense of what a service fee was for. Businesses could not depend on the description of a service to clearly identify bank fees because banks too often describe like-services differently.

Service Detail Summary					
AFP Code	Description	Volume	Unit Price	Service Charge	Balance Equivalent
	* ACH Origination Services				
250000	ACH Origination Module Maintenance	1	50.0000	$ 50.00	$ 325,893

An Active Account?

When doing bank fee monitoring (often referred to as bank fee analysis), one of the first questions to consider is whether this service is being charged for an active account. In account analysis, demand deposit accounts are often closed or no longer used. Unfortunately for businesses, analysis systems sometimes continue to charge recurring fees on such accounts. This is because while the account may be closed in the core deposit system, it isn't always closed in the analysis system. This happens when there is poor integration between these two systems (one doesn't know exactly what the other is doing).

Unless there is some form of bank fee monitoring where the anomaly is caught, such an account could possibly be charged for ongoing maintenance fees indefinitely, even though there is no actual account activity. Analysis systems often establish monthly maintenance fees using instructions calling for the automatic generation of recurring monthly fees. When an analysis account is charged for nothing but recurring fees and no other transaction activity, it is a clear sign that the deposit account at the business in question is likely closed (or inactive) and unless discovered, the recurring maintenance charges will continue to be debited.

Service Properly Identified?

Services appearing on a statement for the very first time typically set off alarms when doing bank fee monitoring and should be cause for concern. This is especially true of recurring maintenance fees which typically are present for all treasury management products. Has the service, as described, ever been seen on this account before? Did this account subscribe to use the ACH Origination service? Both are important questions when analyzing every individual line-item service fee.

Service Properly Coded?

In the example above, it just so happens that AFP Code 250000 is the proper domestic code for *ACH Origination*. The code in this example is shown on the statement for illustration, but that practice is not common. The bank in essence is stating that they believe AFP Code 250000 is the AFP code designed to depict *ACH Origination*. The point being made here is that sometimes banks print (or send) the wrong AFP code to corporate recipients which creates havoc for automated bank fee monitoring systems.

For automated bank fee monitoring systems depending upon electronic transmission of service fee line-items, there is both an AFP Service Code and a Bank Service Identification Code (sometimes referred to as a BSID) defined in the specifications. In other words, a bank is asked to send their own code used to identify a service in conjunction with what they think the AFP Code is. This practice allows automated bank fee monitoring systems to adjust for errant AFP Code assignments.

In other words, Acme Industries Inc. might find that First National Bank is sending an AFP Code of 251000 on their monthly statement file (the wrong AFP Code for ACH Origination Maintenance fee). Acme Industries Inc. uses a premium bank fee monitoring system though, and it knows that for Bank Service ID Code 27 from First National Bank (the bank's code for ACH Origination), the AFP Code is really supposed to be 250000.

Given the bank's BSID - Bank Service ID Code, a premium bank fee monitoring system is able to internally recognize that the AFP Code sent (251000) really should be AFP Code 250000 so all further analysis of price, volume, etc. will have this understanding. This idiosyncrasy is very important in automated bank fee monitoring because many banks simply are not that experienced at mapping their AFP Service Codes for their corporate customers / recipients and often send the wrong code for a line-item service.

Expected Service Volume?

Once a line-item service is properly identified, bank fee monitoring involves analyzing the volume of such a service. Recurring maintenance fees are rather simple in that their volume is typically set to one (1). This simple fact grows in complexity though with relationships of accounts. If Acme Industries, Inc. has a relationship of 20 deposit accounts and 15 of them are using the bank's Online Wire system, the relationship summary statement will likely have a volume of 15 on the relationship summary statement. Bank fee monitoring involves looking at volumes of the past and comparing them to the current volumes. If there is a variance outside of the established guardrails in the bank fee monitoring system, the service would be flagged, and a case likely would be created, calling for human intervention.

> *Advanced bank fee monitoring systems typically have embedded case management tools that create and manage any/all cases created by the monitoring software. These cases are typically prioritized by dollar amounts involved and worked by treasury staff through to resolution.*

Aside from recurring fees in account analysis, most bank fee monitoring systems have the capability of analyzing activity volumes sent by their bank as compared to expected volumes fed into the bank fee monitoring systems daily. In other words, if Acme Industries Inc. keeps track of every *Domestic Wire Transfer* initiated in June 2025, they will likely feed that volume into the bank fee monitoring system via automation so when the June 2025 analysis / billing statement arrives in July, the volume expected by Acme can be compared to the volume on the bank's account analysis statement. Any discrepancy would be cause for the service to be flagged and a case likely would be created. Case management tools will typically identify such a problem with a case type code of some sort. A case representing a volume mismatch is quite different than a case involving recurring fees on an account with no transaction activity.

The key point here is that banks (unintentionally) do make mistakes, errors can occur, and sometimes the commercial billing system is simply dealing with the downstream effect of some external process or some other bank application.

> *In 2010, a Chicago Citibank mistakenly printed the account's social security number on the outside of 600k customer envelopes when sending year-end tax statements. Do you doubt for one second, that a bank possibly may not be charging the correct volume on any of their treasury management services?*

CHICAGO, March 9 (UPI) -- A Chicago Citibank mailed year-end tax statements to 600,000 customers that included the customers' Social Security numbers, bank officials said.

Citibank said the letters sent in late January with Social Security numbers on the outside of the envelopes was a processing error, the Chicago Tribune reported.

Reasonable Service Fee?

Service fees in bank fee monitoring are scrutinized in numerous ways, not the least of which is contracted pricing. How each service fee is looked at will vary depending upon the type of service fee involved (e.g. a volume-based service with a unit price vs. a flat fee service having no volume involved). When volumes are involved as is the case most often, bank fee monitoring will most always include checking the basic math on the statement because the volume shown * the unit price should = the service fee. Any error in basic math would certainly cause a service to be flagged and a case created. The focus quickly turns to unit price for volume-based services.

Bank fee monitoring systems commonly store what I call *promised* pricing. If a corporate RFP comes back from a bank and the bank is stipulating the *Checks Paid* service will be $0.20 per/check, the corporate treasury team will want to ensure this pricing hasn't changed on the monthly analysis statement over time. If the price on the statement does change, it certainly would be important to know if the bank reserved the right to make such a change for the account.

Contract Pricing

Contract pricing is often used with premium account analysis solutions (and bank fee monitoring systems). With contract pricing, there is typically an effective date and an expiration date for service pricing where the price is typically frozen for the agreed upon timeframe (that is the intent anyway). Most bank fee monitoring systems will take contract pricing into consideration before flagging any service and creating a case related to the pricing problem.

It is important to note that while banking fees are highly regulated for consumer accounts and advance notices of change are often required for compliance purposes, there are no such rules for commercial accounts. When it comes to commercial billing, a bank can pretty much do whatever they want with their pricing. The concept of contract pricing is beneficial to the corporate treasurer because it becomes a guardrail against future change. It also helps a corporate treasury department with accurate budgeting for their bank fees, yet another reason for doing bank fee monitoring in the first place.

Summary

In this chapter I have described how bank fee monitoring might be done on a single service. Imagine the complexity of analyzing numerous services on numerous accounts within a complex billing relationship. The same could be said for account balances, earnings allowance calculations, etc. Now that you know the nature of what bank fee monitoring is looking for, in the next chapter I will describe different approaches to doing bank fee monitoring, as one size doesn't fit all.

Thirteen

Bank Fee Monitoring – One Size Doesn't Fit All

Overview

When a business of any size considers a workflow for bank fee monitoring, the best practice is to start with the normal amount of bank fees being dealt with on an annual basis and then apply the 15% error target touted by those with years of experience in doing such monitoring. Clearly, there must be a ROI (Return on Investment) from the processes and procedures put into place. Nobody wants to spend $10k in real dollars in search of what *might possibly* be $10k in bank fee errors. Having a general idea of a business's bank fees can then drive decision making on what approach to take each month, when it comes to analyzing the bank fees.

The following describes how bank fee analysis would likely change with various types / sizes of businesses. As outlined in the previous chapter, regarding what can possibly be wrong, the details surrounding possible errors don't really change. It is the process that one will need to go through that will change based upon the amount of fees and volume of account analysis statements / services involved.

I've outlined four categories of treasury customers below and segmented them by approximately how much in bank fees they pay annually. The amounts themselves are not as important as the fact that there likely is four different categories, and from a bank fee monitoring perspective, each would be handled quite differently.

Micro Business

When it comes to account analysis, I define a Micro Business as a very small business account that does not use ANY treasury management services. An account like this is likely paying under $500 annually in banking fees. Honestly, we seldom see such accounts in commercial account analysis & billing systems. They are sometimes present though, usually when a financial institution decides to do all their business account billing from within a single billing platform. These businesses (sometimes referred to as mom & pop businesses) normally don't receive account analysis statements, even if they are billed by the account analysis system.

Basically, there is little to monitor with these accounts. Service charges would be minimal even if present, and the time it would take to implement any bank fee monitoring procedures regarding these types of accounts would hardly be worth it. Banks that do have Micro Businesses on the analysis system seldom produce and deliver a billing statement, which itself is a costly process for the bank. Who would spend the money on a postage stamp, to deliver a bill for one dollar?

Small Business

The delineation for Small Business Accounts here is that the account is using at least one treasury management service and the billing for such is being done in the analysis system. If I could generalize a bit, these accounts typically pay under $2,500 in bank fees annually. I often advise banks to look for this differentiation in their business accounts and make sure the small businesses using treasury services are put on account analysis. The primary reason for this is that the bank's treasury management billing is all performed from within a single system vs. charging some accounts from within the core deposit system and other accounts in the analysis system. Having all treasury services billed from one system makes it possible to create the likes of revenue trend analysis because the system sees everything. Imagine trying to put a revenue trend analysis together from two different billing systems.

Even when in the account analysis system, Small Business accounts don't always have an analysis statement generated. If there are no analysis statements, there cannot possibly be any bank fee analysis afterwards. The truth here is that even if there is an analysis statement for a Small Business account, it would normally involve a visual approach to bank fee monitoring. A person would simply look at the statement and ask themselves; Is this my account? Is this a service I signed up for? Does the volume look correct? Does the price look correct? Does the charge make sense given the volume and the price?

A Small Business account with an analysis statement is very simple in nature because there are generally few treasury services. These accounts typically do not have an earnings credit rate assigned to them so there is no earnings allowance to offset service fees. If any balances are even shown on such a statement, it would typically be because some banks offer discounts (or waivers) when certain average balances (or minimum balances) are maintained. For any such deals, banks need to put the balances on the statements so the customers can see why something was charged or waived.

Middle Market

This business category is being identified here for all businesses that are larger than the Small Business accounts defined above but are paying less than $250k annually in bank fees. As you can tell, that is a very wide breadth of accounts. This business category uses lots of treasury management services where it would be difficult or error prone to rely on purely a visual approach to bank fee monitoring. Unfortunately, the visual approach to bank fee monitoring is what most of these businesses do today.

I use the $250k upper fee level because that is the level of annual bank fees a company is going to be dealing with before considering a completely automated approach to bank fee monitoring using a 3rd party vendor software system. If you apply the 15% error rate (which in many cases could be on the high side), a business paying $250k annually is probably looking for errors valued at about $3k in monthly bank fees, [($250k X 15%) / 12 Months]. A vendor's automated software solution can easily cost $3k per/month for a business to use. Again, who wants to spend $3k in actual dollars each month to find $3k in potential billing problems that could not be found visually? The ROI simply isn't there when a business is paying less than $250k annually. Every vendor solution has different pricing schemes, so I am sharing approximations here that need to be considered.

For years, businesses in this category have been pleading with their bank to provide an analysis statement with all the line item services and fees in a digital format like MS Excel. Given a digital version of the line-item services each month, a middle market business could use the service description (or even better the AFP code) for a service, to look up what the company has recorded as the actual price they should be paying for the service. Using a spreadsheet approach then, the business analyst could do a line-by-line verification of the bank fees each month. Once again, the business could verify all the basic facts for the service; Is this a service I signed up for? Does the volume look correct? Does the price match my records? Does the charge make sense given the volume and the price? With a digital version of their bank fees, a business could electronically verify their analysis statement vs. visually.

While beyond the scope of bank fee monitoring, a business given the monthly details related to banks fees could also generate some rather interesting visualizations of these fees as well. This would typically be done for internal management reporting and budgeting. Part IV of this guide goes into more detail regarding the digitalization of bank fees and illustrates other possibilities with this detailed data firmly in the hands of the companies who are paying the fees.

Domestic and International Corporate Treasury

This account category normally includes large corporations dealing with enormous amounts of bank fees where the scrutiny of such fees becomes very important. I've listed $250k in annual fees as a floor for this category but this floor value could be considered higher by some. Take for example, a business with an MS Excel guru who could create some rather comprehensive bank fee monitoring tools using spreadsheet(s) from the bank (or creating spreadsheets from images of the analysis statements). Whatever floor is used, turning to a vendor software solution for automated bank fee analysis though, requires a very strong ROI.

When you imagine a multinational corporation paying $2.5m in bank fees annually, you very quickly realize the need for bank fee monitoring. When you find such a business is made up of hundreds of accounts in the organizational structure of the business (not to mention thousands of services), you understand the need for an automated approach to the bank fee analysis process.

Automation surrounding any bank fee monitoring solution is driven by electronic (digital) files representing account analysis statements. Automated solutions ingest these electronic files and perform the analysis. Problems found during bank fee monitoring commonly are handled by the creation of *Problem Cases.* Each case created by fee monitoring is represented by a dollar amount associated with the case. The *Problem Cases* created are looked at individually (a manual process) for resolution. Resolutions to billing issues often mean involving the bank.

Finalizing the bank fee analysis for a given month most often means closing or arriving at a conclusion on all the billing issue cases created in the bank fee monitoring.

Summary

One should be able to ascertain from this chapter that bank fee monitoring is absolutely a necessary process, but size does matter. Money spent in the process of searching for billing problems needs to be justified.

Fourteen

The Digital Files of Bank Fee Monitoring

Bank fee monitoring has only become possible through the decades by the adoption of standards. Both banks and large corporations had to come together and agree upon a standard for how account analysis statements were to be represented and monitored. The banks had to agree, because they were going to be responsible for creating a standard file format that could be understood. Corporations had to agree to the standards, because they were going to be responsible for interpreting the files delivered to them by the banks.

Bank fee monitoring standards didn't develop overnight, it took decades. The initial version of the account analysis electronic file format used domestically went through many changes while further standardization needs outside of the US developed. Today, there are essentially three standard file formats created by banks and ingested into corporate bank fee monitoring systems.

The EDI 822 File Format

In the late 1980's, the Treasury Management Association, known today as the AFP-Association for Financial Professionals, worked with the American National Standards Institute's (ANSI) Accredited Standards Committee (ASC) X12 to develop what is known today as Transaction

Set (TS) 822, the electronic data interchange (EDI) format for transmitting account analysis information.

Service codes used to identify and describe bank services were eventually incorporated into this TS 822 format by the AFP. The use of the AFP service code made it possible for corporations to compare services from different banks. The initial versions of TS 822 were very fluid and constantly updated with version numbers. The most common version of TS 822 today was originally released in December of 1997 and known as version 4010 which means version 4, release 1.

Today, this file format is commonly referred to as an *822 file* in the treasury management industry and has most notably become the domestic standard for the transmission of commercial account analysis and billing statements.

While it is a text file format, an 822 file is not readable by an untrained observer. The EDI 822 file format is, by design, meant to be ingested into software applications that parse the data, deciphering it for bank fee monitoring.

> *As a computer programmer back in the late 1980's, I was handed one of the most difficult challenges of my entire career. After endless hours, I eventually created and sold one of the very first software applications ever built, to create the new EDI 822 file format for banks. The application back then was known as "The 822 Express".*

As years passed on, 822 file adoption increased but weaknesses in the ANSI 822 standards / format began to surface. The 822 standards did not support multiple currencies. It also did not support the international taxation of bank services. These shortcomings in the 822 standards led to the creation of an entirely new and different electronic format.

The TWIST BSB File Format

An organization known as TWIST - Transaction Workstation International Standards Team developed an entirely new global standard for account analysis. They had plenty of advice from corporations, bankers, and software technicians. TWIST created what became known as the TWIST BSB (Bank Services Billing) standard in late 2006. This file format was XML based (extensible markup language) and used every bit of the data defined by the 822 standards. The TWIST BSB, however, also included support for multiple currencies as well as support for the taxation of banking services.

Adoption of the new TWIST standard was very slow and through time, it became clear that although it became a global standard for commercial billing, it lacked the ability to relate international services to US based services. Essentially, the industry needed a complete revamping of the AFP Service Codes to accomplish this.

Contemplating the possibility of yet another standard, a group of banks and corporations together involved the AFP and the International Standards Organization (ISO) to try and resolve any/all issues with the TWIST BSB global standard and come up with an ISO certified solution.

The TWIST BSB is still in use today and supported by many banks, software vendors, and corporations.

The ISO 20022 File Format

Given an effort to develop an ISO certified standard for account analysis, the AFP-Association for Financial Professionals developed a new set of common, global service codes to be used in the new standard. Now, the new ISO 20022 BSB global electronic statement standard, known as "camt.086", is fully documented and available on the ISO web page.

The camt.086 was accepted by the ISO20022 standard and since its inception in 2012 there have now been 3 versions. The CGI-MP Working Group 5 reviews the camt.086 schema on a regular basis to determine whether updates are needed. Other updates may be required due to changes to the overall ISO20022 standard.

Today, the "camt.086" is the international standard for electronic account analysis and bank fee monitoring.

PART IV: The Road Ahead

As we look to the future and wonder what is in store for commercial account analysis and bank fee monitoring, I think it is important to understand the past and what significant events through the years brought us to here.

1987

First Publication of TMA Account Analysis Standard. TMA Codes designed for Services Only and are 6 characters in length. The first two characters of the TMA Service Code depict the product category.

1993

TMA Codes Revised. In addition to service codes, TMA Codes for Balances & Compensation Information Developed

1997

TMA Service Codes Revised and Expanded, TMA Codes for Balances & Compensation Information Standardised

1998

TMA Guide to Account Analysis Published the *Statement Standards and Transaction Set 822 Implementation Guide (aka. The Green Book)*

2005

TWIST announces baseline version of the requirements document and the XML schema

2006

TWIST releases 3.1 version of the BSB electronic standard. BSB is conceptually the global equivalent to the ANSI 822. Essentially a superset of the 822. BSB includes virtually all the substantive business requirements and capabilities found in the 822. BSB accommodates multi-currency and value added tax, features not found in 822

2007

Very first bank goes live with the TWIST BSB. BSB accommodates multi-currency and value added tax, features not found in 822

2008

AFP publishes Global Service Codes to standardize service item identification

2009

A new version of the TWIST BSB is published by ISO 20022 (camt.086)

2011

The Dodd-Frank Wall Street Reform and Consumer Protection Act makes it legal for banks to pay interest on business checking accounts. CGI-MP forms Work Group 5 to harmonise use of the ISO 20022 BSB standard

2012

A new version of the BSB standard is published (ISO 20022 camt.086 version 2), enhanced to include support for ISO 20022 Bank Transaction Codes

2020

Elimination of the standard 10% Reserve Requirement reduction in account analysis

2022

AFP Task Force adds new product categories and makes changes to almost 70% of all AFP Service Codes

One of the conclusions one can take from an event history like this is that account analysis itself hasn't changed too much, but the digitalization of all the information surrounding account analysis has weathered quite a storm.

This digitalization and standardisation of information has now opened the door for more software vendors to enter the market of account analysis products (for banks) and bank fee monitoring products (for corporate treasury).

In the chapters that follow, I share my own vision for where I am seeing commercial account analysis going from here.

Fifteen

Bank Fee Connectivity

The Digitalization of Commercial Service Fees

Shouldn't the digital transformation of commercial services include the primary components of accounts analysis and treasury management / bank service fees for any business account? It doesn't make sense to me that John Smith can download his checking account activity into his money management application on his phone but XYZ Property Management, Inc. (where John pays his HOA fees), cannot get the detail line-item entries of the treasury management service fees paid each month, in a similar digital format.

Large corporate entities learned long ago that detailed bank fee data (in digital form) would be required to do bank fee monitoring. Sending a statement image to one of these corporations was never going to be acceptable simply because there was too much data to analyze.

Keep in mind there are multiple possibilities of something being wrong with a single bank fee, starting with "should the service fee being assessed, be on the analysis statement in the first place". Consider a business with multiple deposit accounts in a relationship where one of those accounts is being assessed maintenance fees only. This loner account doesn't exactly stick out in a relationship analysis of 10 deposit accounts and 30 pages of bank fees.

The problem of not having digitized bank service fees was solved for large corporate entities by using special electronic file formats known as the EDI Transaction Set 822 File (Domestic standard) or the XML based camt.086 file (International standard). Both banks and corporate treasurers pay additional fees for the manufacturing, delivery, download, and ingestion of these file formats. Having such data allows the corporations to do bank fee monitoring, to help them verify service charge accuracy. Storing this information over time provides the corporations with needed fee trends, variances, and budgeting information.

Bank Fee Monitoring

Software to create the previously mentioned file formats is complex, software to ingest / process these files is even more complex and most often too costly for smaller businesses to justify.

If banks could connect their treasury management service fees to their customers as they have done with downloadable checking account data, businesses of all sizes could do bank fee monitoring. In fact, banks could change the entire customer experience when it comes to account analysis service fees. With access to the bank fee data, businesses could monitor their bank fees in total, see the trends by month, or monitor their fees by product family / category (ACH, RDC, etc.). Imagine drilling into total fees by month to see the total for each subsidiary product family. Drilling further into Product Families could show service line details.

The challenge for commercial services is to take the image of a service fee from the printed statement (or statement image) and make the details available for customers to view however they want, even download in .CSV format for further analysis. By connecting businesses to their bank fees digitally, banks open numerous possibilities. What a tremendous service offering for business customers. Simply stated, account analysis data should be available from banks in a .CSV format. Delivery of analysis data in .CSV format is probably something a business would pay a monthly fee for. Banks often charge a penalty fee for customers who insist on paper statement delivery. Ironically a .CSV file can turn a penalty fee into a value-added service fee.

When we look back over the previous 20 years, online banking has completely changed the way consumers interact with their checking accounts. Isn't it now time for banks to change the way ALL businesses interact with their Treasury Management Service Fees? IMHO: Yes, this service must be in the future of account analysis. In fact, it is long overdue.

Sixteen

Artificial Intelligence

Using Data Science & AI To Identify Opportunity

If you have ever glanced at an Account Analysis statement you might have found the complexity to be a bit intimidating. Let's face it, terms like "Collected Balance Required" and "Non-Compensable Services" are not terms we hear every day. There is no wonder why the AFP sponsors annual educational sessions on decoding account analysis statements at their national conference. If you were to take some time to see through the complexity of this monthly report (which is what an account analysis statement really is), you would be surprised to find that you could ascertain quite a bit of information about your business customer.

I believe you must first understand that all the information on the account analysis report is collected and brought together from several different areas within a bank. This gathering of information repeats itself every month. Once this information is all collected and presented, anyone looking at the report will get to see all the activity for the customer.

When you think about it, it is hard to believe that existing processes within every bank with commercial accounts are already gathering and collecting information on business accounts, bringing it all together, sorting it into a logical and presentable fashion, and then making the entire report available to those who care to see it.

Service fees related to ACH Origination, Wire Transfer, Lockbox, etc. all originate in these various departments of a bank and typically are shown in separate sections of an analysis statement. These sections are often referred to as product categories. These product categories typically have several service line-items within them.

Visualize a small business customer that is being charged a service fee for two (2) *International Wire Transfers*. A single service like this on an analysis report would certainly make you wonder what sort of business this customer is running. Most billing system vendors make this analysis data available for month over month review. Would it mean anything if the *International Wire Transfers* showing up on the analysis statement have never been seen before? Or if they happen to be on the statement every month?

What can you learn from a statement where the customer is being charged for six hundred thirty-seven (637) *Paid Checks* this month? Does the same statement show any fees for a *Check Positive Pay* service? Such a situation might point to an opportunity to sell the customer on the idea of a Positive Pay Service. Suffice to say that analysis statements show us what a customer is doing, but they also show us what a customer is not doing. Developing service correlations can then point us to direct hits in terms of sales leads. A customer with many deposited items brought into the branch, but no RDC clearly seems to be a candidate for RDC.

The analysis statement can also show customer anomalies as well. What if a statement showed a monthly recurring fee for Remote Deposit Capture but there were not any RDC Item fees on the statement?

Could it be the customer is not using their RDC Service? What if a customer had a subscription fee for Online Banking on the statement but is choosing to do wires manually at the branch instead? Would it be of value to know exactly who these customers are?

The analysis statement shows all the things a customer is doing and what they are not doing. I am not sure there is a better document that could help a bank with knowing more about a customer. While KYC may be a mandate in the industry, from a treasury management sales perspective the analysis statement should be the driving force behind KYO (Know Your Opportunity).

With the development of AI tools to search through the basements of account analysis data, I foresee the day a treasury salesperson will come to work, sign into their analysis system, and see a dashboard of the five (5) customers they should call right now because the data tells us they need to sign up for a fraud protection service. If the salesperson is not yet educated in the bank's fraud protection services, they will one day be able to pull down a list of product categories, choose a different category like Remote Deposit Capture, and instantly see the top five (5) customers (along with their contact information) who are the very best candidates for such.

Call it artificial intelligence or call it data science, whatever you call it, the answers to impactful questions like these, lie in the historical data of account analysis.

Seventeen

Calculations to Come

A Transition to Transaction Fees

I cannot begin to count how many times I said to myself, "okay now I have seen everything when it comes to commercial billing". Just when you think you've seen it all, something new appears on the horizon. I will preface this chapter by stating that account analysis systems have forever been aggregators. In other words, they count the occurrence of transaction items so that a charge can be developed for all the items at the end of a given month.

Of course, there are many different counts that are aggregated in analysis. Aggregation is normally based upon the type of transaction being counted. Credits, debits, deposited items, etc. are all kept track of separately. Service charges for these counts over time, have affectionately become known as P*V items, a simple way of saying "Price * Volume".

Service charge calculations though, sometimes use dollar amounts at the end of a month as the basis for a calculated charge. Using an amount to calculate a charge is not quite as simple as P*V. For example, analysis systems almost from the beginning of time have been able to calculate what used to be referred to as an *FDIC charge*.

This charge to a bank's customer was intended to pass on the bank's cost of their deposit insurance assessment from the FDIC. The fee was typically based upon how many units of $1,000 an account had at the end of a month.

> *Someone along the way had the brilliant idea of looking at units of $100 instead because the calculation slightly increased the calculated service charge, meaning more revenue for the bank.*

Back in 2012, the FDIC ordered banks to stop calling this fee an FDIC charge. So, banks made up obscure names like *Deposit Assessment Fee* or *Balance Maintenance Fee*. The point is that the service calculations were not based on some number of transactions but instead on the account's ledger balance.

Another balance-based service charge found in analysis is the Uncollected Funds Fee. Analysis statements commonly show uncollected funds charges based upon an account's average negative collected balance and a *loan like* interest rate (normally prime + 3% or 4%).

Suffice to say that most billing systems could always calculate service charges based upon P*V and / or month end balances (even average balances). In more than fifty years now, I have never seen a system that would focus on a specific debit / credit transaction on a given day and calculate a single analysis service charge for that transaction and then show it on the analysis statement. The reason is this, analysis systems have always been month end billing systems. The calculations have always been for the aggregated values of transactions and balances over the entire month.

Enter Instant Payments

Account analysis systems everywhere are seemingly going to have to come up with new calculations and new standard display methods (on analysis statements) for transactions known as instant payments. The reason for this much needed change requires an explanation.

Very similar to ACH transactions, instant payments represent different payment modalities and are run on their own individual payment rails. As of the date of this publication, there are principally two instant payment rails being used. RTP (Real Time Payments) is a network built by The Clearing House and was the first instant payment rail to be constructed. More recently, FedNow is another instant payment rail created by the federal reserve. Both the RTP and FedNow standards are based upon ISO 20022 and the two payment rails are very similar in nature.

With the rails constructed now enter the software vendors and tools. Instant payments can be made anytime, anywhere, 365 days a year, and create immediate availability of funds in a customer's checking account (well, within five seconds anyway). Banks across the country can sign up for either RTP, FedNow, or both rails. These subscriptions come with costs though and banks need to be able to pass these costs on to those customers using this new infrastructure.

The instant payment rails present all sorts of use cases for how payments can be made and received instantly. From the real estate industry to the automotive industry, banks are making it possible for businesses to move money instantaneously in a safe and secure manner using RTP and FedNow. Imagine a ride share driver receiving payment from his employer as soon as a passenger slams the door and leaves the vehicle. How about a car loan being approved at a dealership on Sunday afternoon and the necessary funds disbursed to the dealership so the new car owner can drive their new car off the lot immediately.

While banks are slowly implementing this instant payment infrastructure, they are struggling with how they are going to monetize these transactions and pass their costs onto the businesses that are using them. When it comes to billing for these transactions, bankers have come to realize if they are not careful with pricing instant payments, they could hurt other aspects of their treasury management revenue. If a business is paying the bank $25 to send a wire today but sending an instant payment can accomplish the very same task for $1.50, the wire revenue at a bank is going to be greatly affected.

Similar billing dilemmas have arisen with Same Day ACH. The answer to these pricing problems means straying away from the traditional methods of P*V at the end of the month. The answer lies in the ability to look at the individual transaction (in this case an instant payment) and then make the determination what the fee for that transaction should be. An argument can easily be made for a higher fee based upon the amount of a single transaction. Afterall, the RTP network allows transactions to be as high as $1m globally.

Minimums and Maximums

If the billing process for an instant payment has line of site to the individual transaction amount, one could assess a transaction fee in account analysis based upon a percentage of the payment amount. Further then, the calculation could be protected by using a minimum fee and maximum fee guardrail to control the calculation. To not destroy an existing revenue stream from the wire transfer department, instant payments could be competitively priced using this approach. In this case, the use case would define the payment modality vs. a cost savings of one transaction type vs. another.

The unusual part of such a calculation in account analysis is that at the end of a month when all the accumulators are passed for billing, we don't normally see the original transaction detail that the counters are made up of. To calculate a charge based upon a percentage of a single transaction amount and then apply a minimum / maximum guardrail to the charge, means account analysis is going to need access to the individual daily transactions. It is also very likely that account analysis will need to display each of the transactions and the charges associated with each one so that a customer can clearly see why their instant payments amounted to possibly hundreds of dollars in fees at the end of the month.

Summary of Calculations to Come

Creating service charges from item counts and even balances has worked quite well for over 50 years in account analysis. The calculations built into the analysis systems across the nation have absolutely survived quite a long time. It is time for change though, and we can likely thank instant payments (and maybe even same day ACH). The AFP will likely want to become involved and determine how the calculations for individual transaction fees should be displayed on analysis statements. The individual transaction fees are quite different than individual service codes where counts and the like are aggregated.

One probably should look at how such fees might be shown on merchant billing statements because the merchant world has been calculating fees on individual transactions for as long as account analysis has been aggregating counts. Okay, now I have seen everything.

Epilogue/Conclusion

Account Analysis creates an incredible opportunity for any business bank to enhance revenue streams. One cannot look at billing revenue alone though. Profitability Margin, Realization, and Revenue Opportunity Loss are all key performance indicators for financial institutions. Bank Fee Monitoring is very important for any organization paying for bank fees, but size certainly matters.

Hopefully, this book provides insight as to how anyone can eventually arrive at a point where the financial institution is generating clear, concise, and accurate account analysis results. Businesses paying such fees expect that of their financial institutions.

Treasury products need to be paid for so collecting fee income in a fair and efficient manner is well understood by both financial institutions and corporate treasury. As I often say, “Only the air blows for free”.

Appendix A: RFP Questions of Importance

Security Questions

Does your solution support a SAML 2.0 single sign on feature to access your application?

> *SAML (Security Assertion Markup Language) 2.0 is an open standard for single sign on across domains. SAML allows a user to authenticate in one system and then gain access in another system like account analysis, by providing proof of the original authentication. Simply said, it makes life easier for users, so they don't have to maintain separate user ID's and passwords for every system they work with, including account analysis.*

Hosted software processing models referred to as ASP solutions are often used to host legacy applications originally designed & developed for desktop usage (MS Windows Desktop Applications). ASP environments have become a home for such desktop applications and allows them to be served via the internet using 3rd party services (e.g. Citrix). Third party services introduce additional costs, ongoing maintenance, end-user client plug-in software, and additional layers of technology. Would you say that your hosted account analysis solution is completely browser-based (meaning there are no legacy windows desktop components that require special user access via terminal server software or plug-ins)?

The treasury management sales officers need to be able to access the account analysis solution to perform ad-hoc queries and create ad-hoc reports for a variety of reasons. Does your account analysis solution allow our Treasury Management Sales Officers to access the analysis system via the web browser to create their own ad-hoc queries and reports?

> ***Note:** Some account analysis systems have ad-hoc reporting tools that were not designed for the web, so only certain users have access to terminal server software for access to what is essentially a client server application, to do ad-hoc reporting.*

Operational Questions

If an account analysis billing file is securely sent to your FTP server, would it automatically be processed and posted to our account analysis database without any human intervention or handling whatsoever?

If our bank uploads a service billing file containing line-item services and volumes, does your system support the use of different effective dates for each of the line-item services that are in a single file?

Once billing files have all been processed and it is time to generate the account analysis results for the month, can this process be launched automatically based upon scheduling, without any human intervention or button pushing whatsoever?

Once billing files have all been processed and preliminary analysis results are complete, our bank staff sometimes make changes and corrections to customer settings, affecting the account analysis results. Using your solution, would most such changes automatically recalculate the preliminary account analysis results without any human intervention or button pushing whatsoever?

After our bank's preliminary analysis is complete, sometimes service billing files are transmitted late and need to be processed. Once such files are processed, does your account analysis solution automatically recalculate the preliminary account analysis results for all accounts affected by such billing files, without any human intervention or button pushing whatsoever?

Once the billing process for a month is complete and it is time to generate the account analysis statement file(s) for the month, can this process be launched automatically based upon account analysis finalization scheduling, without any human intervention or button pushing whatsoever?

Once the billing process for a month is complete and it is time to generate account debits (credits) to send to the core demand deposit system, can this process be launched automatically based upon the analysis finalization scheduling, without any human intervention or button pushing whatsoever?

Once the billing process for a month is complete and it is time to send analysis data to our data warehouse, can this process be launched automatically based upon analysis finalization scheduling, without any human intervention or button pushing whatsoever?

Once the billing process for a month is complete and all the data has been sent to our data warehouse, sometimes the analysis results are changed & recalculated. If a customer analysis is completely re-done for a month in the past, does that updated data for the month in question automatically get sent to our data warehouse?

> *If your bank depends solely upon a data warehouse for management reporting, I cannot over emphasize the importance of this question. Best practice for standard management reporting is often based upon the data warehouse. If the account analysis system does not stay in daily synchronization with the data warehouse by feeding any/all updates to the warehouse, any such reporting would be subject to stale data possibly causing errant results. Some account analysis systems are designed to feed analysis results to the data warehouse once a month, when the end of month close process is finished. The problem with this approach is that results from account analysis (or even something as simple as pricing) can change daily.*

When a New Account is opened in our Demand Deposit System and we designate it to be sent to account analysis, can an account analysis effective date be set for the account billing?

When a New Account is opened in our Demand Deposit System and we designate it to be sent to account analysis, would it normally appear in our account analysis database the next morning, without any human intervention whatsoever?

With your solution, is it a standard operating procedure for daily ending balances in the Demand Deposit System to be sent to the account analysis system each day?

If the answer to the question above is YES, are the average ledger and collected balances automatically recalculated and available for usage in your account analysis solution on any given day of the month?

With your solution, is it a standard operating procedure for daily service activity in the Demand Deposit System to be sent to the account analysis system each day?

If a stand-alone account analysis customer closes their account in the middle of a month, can your analysis solution produce a snapshot statement (statement on demand) showing all deposit system activity to date and a total amount of fees due based upon that activity?

When the account analysis cycle is finalized, does your solution allow for varying debit delay periods so some accounts can be charged (auto debited) right away while other accounts on different processing plans are charged several days after the analysis finalization?

If automatic debiting of fees were to be delayed for some number of days between the finalization of the account analysis and the actual settlement / debiting of our accounts, and then some accounts are changed & re-analyzed during the delay period for whatever reason, would the debit amount automatically be corrected before transmitting to the core Demand Deposit system?

Do you consider your solution to be a *multicurrency* account analysis system?

If your solution is a multicurrency solution, does it support obtaining foreign exchange rates using an API call to a third-party service providing such rates?

Account Feature Questions

Would we be able to set an account feature to automatically WAIVE a New Account after XX number of billing cycles (not actually figuring out an expiration date but just setting XX number of cycles)?

Would we be able to use an account feature that allows us to automatically WAIVE an Account whose Average Ledger Balance exceeded a certain value?

Would we be able to use an account feature that allows us to automatically WAIVE any/all fees over a prescribed amount set for the account (e.g. dynamically waive all fees more than $1,000).

Many account analysis systems just ignore excess earnings allowances when an account on a monthly billing cycle is in an excess position. Does your solution allow us to automatically roll over excess earnings credits for certain accounts while ignoring this excess position on other monthly accounts?

We do not want to roll over excess earnings credits less than $10.00 (or more than $500) on monthly billing accounts. If the answer to the previous question is YES, can we stipulate an amount / limit so that we only roll over excess earnings credits above a specific amount along with a maximum amount to roll over?

We want to keep our database as clean and efficient as possible. If we establish some user defined fields for account analysis, will your solution allow us to pre-define the VALID values that we would allow to appear in those user fields?

If your solution is a multicurrency system, does it support the concept of a deposit account having a different Balance Currency code vs. Settlement or Pricing Currency code?

Account Relationship Structure Questions

Consider the following customer relationship structure as you answer the questions that follow. The relationship structure below shows five (5) levels of account relationships. Can your account analysis solution produce billing statements for each account in a structure such as this?

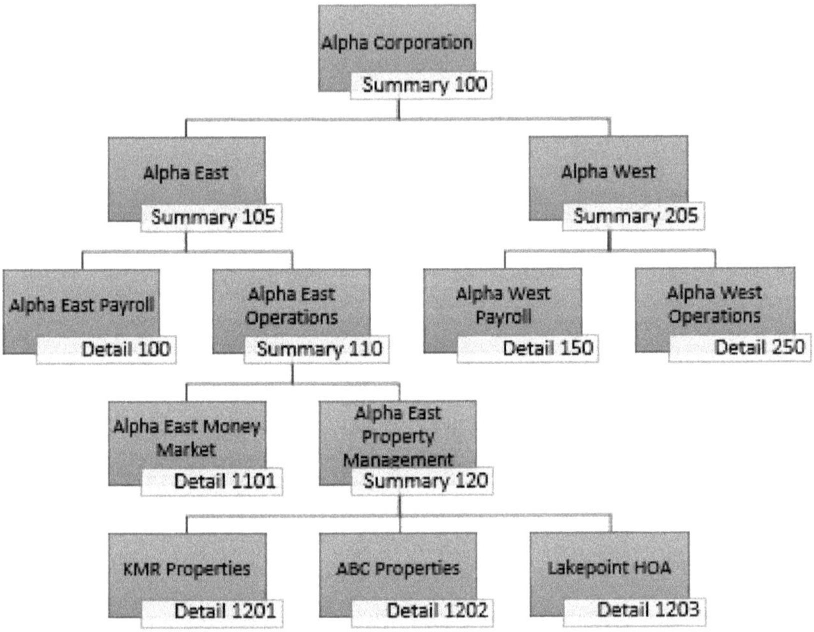

All the account information for *Summary 120 Alpha East Property Management* still needs to roll up to *Summary 100 Alpha Corporation* for summary statement reporting. Can your account analysis solution create the proper summary statements and automatically debit the correct amounts to the correct accounts for this scenario?

The account summary labeled *Summary 120 Alpha East Property Management* is a fully analyzed relationship. This property management organization wants the three (3) detail accounts (1201, 1202, and 1203) to each be automatically debited for two (2) very specific fee-based services (e.g. ACH Positive Pay and Check Positive Pay) while rolling up and analyzing all the remaining service fees. Can your account analysis solution accommodate this need for auto-debiting subsidiary accounts in a property management relationship?

Sometimes customers want statement packages to consist of statements from pieces and parts of an overall analysis relationship. Can your account analysis solution create a statement package for the *Alpha West Payroll* statement and the *Alpha East Payroll* statement and then produce the two together for mailing in a single envelope (to a specific address) in addition to creating these statement pages as a part of the overall statement package for *Alpha Corporation*?

If your solution is a multicurrency system, could the accounts *Alpha West Payroll* and *Alpha West Operations* have their balances stored and displayed using different Currency Codes (USD, CAD, etc.)?

Can your account analysis solution produce a duplicate statement set for an entire relationship of accounts using a simple account setting?

There are five (5) Summary Accounts in this relationship diagram shown above. Summary Accounts in account analysis normally inherit the demographics of one underlying detail account (aka. subsidiary account). This is very important because these demographics often control pricing for summary analysis. Does your account analysis solution allow us to stipulate specifically which subsidiary account to use (because it may not be the *charge to* / debit account) for Summary Account demographic settings?

When subsidiary accounts within a relationship structure have different unit prices for the exact same service, does your account analysis solution show a separate line-item service by distinct unit price on the relationship summary statements (as shown in this example below)?

Treasury Management Services

ACH Origination

ACH Items	5	0.2500	1.25
ACH Items	1	0.4000	.40
ACH Items	3	0.0900	.27

When processing accounts & relationships, we look for draws into uncollected funds and charge our customers for even one day of having a draw into their uncollected funds. For account relationships, we feel the system must look at all the accounts in a relationship (for a single day) to determine if the relationship (customer) drew into uncollected funds on that day. Does your solution allow the entire relationship structure to be considered when looking at a single day of drawing into uncollected funds?

Pricing of Products & Services Questions

Does your solution allow for the setting of a unit cost factor on service line items so that a service margin can be calculated?

Does your solution allow for the use of *Promotional Price Lists* that create concession pricing on new accounts for a specified period of time, and then auto-expires after XX months regardless of when the account was opened?

Does your solution support a concession pricing claw-back feature where concession pricing can automatically be renewed at a higher value / price point based upon a percentage rate (e.g. 1.XX %) of the existing price concession?

Most account analysis solutions have a data field that controls which price list(s) an account might use to calculate analysis results. A field like this might be called an analysis type, a class code, a service charge type, etc. Whatever it is called in your solution, changes to this code are typically very time sensitive because a change like this affects pricing in account analysis. Can changes to a pricing control code like this be effective dated in your solution?

Does your solution support tiered pricing for services where the unit pricing tiers are at least 10 levels deep?

Does your solution support automatic concession pricing for a volume of Customer Deposits (as an example), based upon the total derived volume of any other / group of services?

Our financial institution is considering a packaged discount. If a customer has three (3) or more online services like ACH, RDC, and a Wire Module for example, we want to remove those normal maintenance fees from the statement and charge a single fee for an all-inclusive online banking package instead. Does your solution support automatic product packaging where the presence of two, three, or more services are automatically replaced by a single service and price point as described in this example?

We are considering the use of balance-directed pricing. For example, if a balance is $100,000 or less, the first ten (10) items are free and all other items are $1.00 each; if the balance is over $100,000, the first twenty-five (25) items are free, and the remaining items are $0.90 each. Does your solution support tiered unit pricing for a single service (based upon volumes) but varying price values for this tier, based upon a balance?

If your solution is a multicurrency system, could one account in a relationship have all unit pricing stipulated as USD-US Dollars while another account in the same relationship has all unit pricing stipulated in CAD-Canadian Dollars?

Reporting & Statement Questions

We often need to create ad-hoc reports from account analysis data in the form of Excel spreadsheets. These ad-hoc reports often contain many columns including dates, volumes, currency fields, percentage rates, and more. Some applications create ad-hoc reports like these with the Excel columns all in a text data format making it difficult to add totals, create formulas, or otherwise make good use of the data for charts, graphs, and pivot tables. Does your application create such ad-hoc reports with all the data columns automatically set in their native data format?

Knowing Your Customer (KYC) is very important at our financial institution. Does the reporting from your account analysis solution provide a customer trend view of account analysis balances / results with all the statement data points listed down the left side of the report and the month over month trend values spanning left to right across the report?

Our Billing Files often contain service volumes along with an optional description regarding what the volume is specifically for (e.g. an adjustment, a Lockbox #, etc.). Does your solution allow service descriptions such as this to be printed on the account analysis statement in addition to the basic service description (e.g. Paid Items-Lockbox #12345, etc.)?

Third party vendor fees often have their own service descriptions such as: Dunbar Armored Car Invoice #23456. Can we use descriptions such as this for such line items?

If your solution is a multicurrency system, could I generate a report for all accounts, regardless of their individual Currency Codes, in a single targeted currency?

Glossary

AFP

Association for Financial Professionals. This organization was previously known as the TMA-Treasury Management Association and before that, the National Corporate Cash Management Association (NCCMA).

AFP Service Codes

The industry standard for identifying service charges that appear on account analysis statements and in responding to RFPs. These industry standard codes are assigned by all major banks to their cash management services and billed to large corporations on their account analysis or bank fee statements. These codes are six (6) digits in length where the first two digits identify a product category. Code 05 for example refers to the Lockbox product category of services.

AFP Global Service Codes

These codes were originally published in 2011. The global service codes were designed specifically for the international community, based largely on the original AFP Service Codes created in the U.S. for use in the ASC X12 EDI 822 standard in 1986. The Global AFP Service Codes are accepted in the market as the standardized bank billing code(s) set worldwide. The global service code is 8 characters in length with the first three letters designed to be an acronym for the product family / category. An acronym like "LBX" is often used for lockbox services. The set includes over 1,100 codes for banking services. They are now widely adopted across Europe, the Middle East, Africa and the Pacific Rim. The code set was created specifically for use with the TWIST BSB or CAMT.086 bank billing file format. These service codes also offer industry standard service descriptions for cash management services that are recommended to be used in RFPs.

BSID

Bank Service Identification Code. This code is used to identify a service within a bank's system. It is the same as the BTC.

BTC

Bank Transaction Code. This code is used to identify a service within a bank's system. It is the same as the BSID.

BSB

Bank Services Billing. This acronym is used to describe a billing file format commonly used in the billing of treasury management services. The intent for designing the file format was to create a standard that governs the format of electronic bills or bank fee reporting sent out by financial institutions, to any recipient regardless of country or currency.

BSB File Formats

Currently, there are four available formats. They are TWIST 3.1 Statement Format and CAMT.086.001.01, CAMT.086.001.02, and CAMT.086.001.03. TWIST 3.1 was the first XML BSB statement format developed back in the 2000's. The CAMT.086 format was accepted as an ISO20022 standard.

CAMT.086

An XML based BSB File Format that has become the global international standard, supporting multiple currencies for bank fee reporting.

CGI-MP

Common Global Implementation-Market Practice. This acronym is used to describe a group of banks, corporate treasury practitioners, financial application vendors, and standardizers working to harmonize use of BSB and other standards. Work Group 5 addresses BSB.

ECR

Earning Credit Rate. This rate is used to compute the earnings allowance in account analysis. The earnings allowance is used to offset bank fees, more specifically, compensable bank fees.

EDI

Electronic Data Interchange.

ICR

Interest Credit Rate. This rate is used to compute the interest credit that is paid to an account. Interest credits are often paid to accounts from many banking systems, including account analysis.

ISO 20022

International Standards Organization. Represents the current version of the standard BSB (ISO 20022, camt.086) and related documentation, including the "Message Usage Guide" which describes the data content requirements of the Bank Services Billing (BSB) standard as defined by ISO 20022.

SWIFT

Society for Worldwide Interbank Financial Telecommunication. This is a global financial messaging network used by corporations and banks to transmit data using standard message formats.

TWIST

Transaction Workflow Innovation Standards Team. The organization's focus is to assist in the development of industry standards for treasury management.

Bibliography

Reference to actual AFP Service Codes™ copyrighted by the Association for Finance Professionals. Actual AFP Service Codes referred to are reprinted with permission from the AFP: www.financialprofessionals.org

Hunt, T. AFP Service Codes Accredited Provider Program. Retrieved from https://www.afponline.org/training-resources/resources/afp-service-codes/accredited-provider

Andrules, B. (2018, November 4). AFP Service Codes: The General Ledger Chart of Accounts for Bank Fees. Retrieved from https://www.redbridgedta.com/us/market-intelligence/afp-service-codes-the-general-ledger-chart-of-accounts-for-bank-fees/

Meyer, B. (2023, October 6). Global AFP Service Codes Committee Review. Retrieved from https://www.afponline.org/training-resources/resources/articles/Details/global-afp-service-codes-committee-review

(2010, March 9). Bank prints S.S. numbers on envelope. Retrieved from https://www.upi.com/Top_News/US/2010/03/09/Bank-prints-SS-numbers-on-envelope/60561268167953/

Acknowledgments

In creating this book, I wanted to get down on to paper, everything I have learned and experienced first-hand throughout my career, as it relates to commercial account analysis. I feel like I have accomplished my goal, but what is missing in the pages of this book are the names of so many people I've engaged with and learned from along the way.

I am going to first and foremost acknowledge my wife Peg who has always been encouraging and supportive of me in the work that I do. Her support and encouragement have always been fuel for my flight. Whenever I start flying too high, she always brings me back closer to ground level, and without a discouraging word. Peg has always made me believe that anything is possible. Whenever there is anything that I wanted to do or try, she always says "*just go for it*". Conversely, whenever she sees me frown, she just looks at me and says, "*snap out of it*".

Peg has been a tremendous role model for me too, having become an expert herself in the travel industry, with her own travel business franchise of more than 20 years. Still today, the enthusiasm I overhear in her phone conversations sound to me like she is talking with her very first customer.

I would be remiss, not to mention both Steve and Pat Weiland, who have been an inspiration to me for more years than they'll ever know. As a former IBM Systems Engineer back in the 1960's, Steve taught me all about computer programming in IBM Assembler Language (BAL) and Demand Deposit Accounting within a bank. Back in the 1970's when I first met Steve, he would code programs, test them, sell them, and then go install them. Watching and learning from his actions, how could I not be amazed? Later in life Steve introduced me to the MS-DOS based QuickBasic programming language. Steve and Pat Weiland together, asked me to create what became known as "*The 822 Express*" using this new technology at the time.

Soon after the launch of "*The 822 Express*", both Steve and Pat placed an enormous amount of trust in me by having me re-write and improve what had then become an old account analysis system containing many limitations. The system was originally mainframe based (known as APEX) but was converted to QuickBasic (green screens) and brought to market as APX-PC.

My challenge was to take all this and turn everything into one of the first Microsoft Windows based commercial account analysis systems known to the industry. Truth be told, my life turned into coding, testing, selling, and implementing account analysis solutions across the nation, only to then rinse and repeat the process more than 100 times at different banks through two decades. I never could have written this book without having the experiences originally afforded to me by Steve and Pat Weiland.

Bill Andrules is the former managing director of the Commercial Account Analysis team at The Weiland Financial Group, Inc. and the principal author of the original Microsoft Windows based, Weiland Account Analysis System. As a software developer, he also authored one of the very first applications to ever deliver the account analysis statement electronically via the ASC X12 / EDI transaction set 822. The application was then known as "The 822 Express" and although it's evolved into a new name, the programming is still being used today by some of the nation's largest financial institutions.

Bill is currently a Sales Engineer / Product Sales Consultant with a industry leading core system provider representing Account Analysis systems. He has spent 50+ years in design, development, marketing, implementation, and support of Account Analysis solutions.

In 1973 Bill studied computer programming languages (IBM BAL, Cobol, and RPG) going to school part time at the College of Lake County in Gurnee, IL. Ironically, he returned to the same college some 25 years later as an instructor himself, and taught Microsoft Visual Basic programming. Through time, Bill ended up hiring seven of his best students to join development teams working on account analysis systems.

In 2009, Bill formed a Commercial Account Analysis & Billing User Group on LinkedIn where he posts newsletters, articles, and offers insight into many areas of account analysis. The treasury professional user group currently has 350+ registered members.

Bill resides in Wellington, FL with his wife Peg, a travel agency franchise owner & herself an expert in her industry for more than twenty years. In his spare time, Bill enjoys both freshwater & saltwater fishing, playing golf, and of course, travel!

www.ingramcontent.com/pod-product-compliance
Lightning Source LLC
LaVergne TN
LVHW050910210926
848482LV00012B/392